RECESSION...
and all that

INFLATION
RECESSION...
and all that

Robert S. Ozaki

Holt, Rinehart and Winston, Inc.
New York   Chicago   San Francisco   Atlanta
Dallas   Montreal   Toronto   London   Sydney

330
O99i

Copyright © 1972 by Holt, Rinehart and Winston, Inc.
All rights reserved
Library of Congress Catalog Card Number: 77-184110
ISBN 0-03-088520-5
Printed in the United States of America
2 3 4 5 065 9 8 7 6 5 4 3 2 1

To Cecilia

PREFACE

This is an informal introduction to economics, intended to expose its central ideas and show that economics can serve as a useful mode of thinking through which we can look at and analyze certain problems of man and society.

I have avoided the use of statistical tables, charts, footnotes and jargon. My concern is not to burden the reader with technical details of the subject but rather to bring out and discuss, in concise language, some of the basic concepts and issues of economics for those who wish to have a taste of the discipline.

I have written this book, imagining that I were having a dialogue with a wide variety of people—students, businessmen, housewives, public administrators, radicals, conservatives, ministers, the semi-retired, the totally retired—who are curious about economics.

For those who feel that the already concise chapters are not concise enough, each chapter is summed up by a verse composed in the style of free haiku.

A Guide to Basic Economics Texts and Suggested Readings are provided at the end of the book to assist the reader interested in further study.

R. S. O.
Berkeley, California

CONTENTS

INFLATION RECESSION...
and all that

1.

A FREE LUNCH FOR ANYONE?

Nothing is more blissful than getting something free. Unfortunately, we must learn at the outset that there is no such thing as a free good. This lesson is very important to economists because, if everything we desire and consume is available without a cost, then there is no need to *economize* on what we buy and use. Economics, which is the study of how to go about *economizing*, loses its *raison d'etre*. The American Economic Association must be dissolved, and college professors teaching macroeconomics as well as the economics of the mackerel canning industry will be obliged to look for new jobs.

Nikita Khrushchev, while still in power, once said, "In the near future Russian workers will be having free lunches." This statement is either sheer rhetoric or total nonsense. Lunches are made of foods. Most foods should be cooked. Someone has to ship foods from farms to kitchens in industrial plants. Foods are grown by farmers who in turn must pay for fertilizers and equipment. So, when Mr. Khrushchev says, "Russian workers will be eating free meals," just what does he mean? The farmers will not be paid for the foods they produce? The only feasible way to give the workers free meals is not to pay a ruble to the cooks, delivery men, farmers, suppliers of fertilizers, and all the others who have worked to produce lunches for the industrial workers. To use socialist jargon, this is a system of "exploiting" many groups of Russians for the benefit of one group. Whatever he meant, it was bad economics.

Every object we desire is not free because it is available only in a finite quantity. Every object we demand is scarce because the supply of resources that must be used to produce it is limited. The only world of free goods is an Alice's Wonderland. A place where you have only to name a thing you want, for instance a bag of peanuts, and push a button, then instantaneously a bag of peanuts appears in front of your nose. But this is magic, not economics.

All goods and services bear varying costs because men and women have worked at different stages of production in order to make them available for you, using raw materials that were in turn produced by some other people. All these people involved in producing what you desire ought to be paid for their work. If you do not pay for your foods, the farmers will stop producing except for their own consumption. With no food you will begin to starve, and out of desperation you will soon be offering a price for the food you partake.

Some goods are terribly expensive (a Boeing 747, an Apollo rocket), some others are moderately costly (a fish tank, a pair of hot pants), yet some others are very cheap but not quite costless (a toothpick, city water). All these costs in modern society are expressed in some monetary units (dollars and cents). We pay the money costs of things we get out of our money income. Some of you may then be tempted to think that we can make things costless by abolishing the use of money. You reason, "if there is no money, there will be no *money* cost, hence there will be no cost to anything." Unfortunately, this would not do the trick. You do not solve the problem by changing the name of the problem.

We are conditioned to think of costs in money terms. Because of this conditioning we often fail to perceive a cost unless it is expressed in dollars and cents. Money, however, is merely a device to measure something else—a surface matter rather than the substance. Cost is, in essence, something you must give up in order to get something else. The truth of the matter is, money or no money, you don't get anything for nothing. If you get something for nothing from someone else, it is free to *you* because someone else is absorbing the cost for you.

If you live in a moneyless world, the cost of things you get must necessarily be paid *in kind*. Your wife has borne a baby, and you pay the midwife from the next village with two chickens. Because your wife cannot work in the fields for the next ten days, you hire a helper to harvest the crop by offering him a bottle of wine per day. Two chickens and a bottle of wine per day are the costs of the services you acquire—something you give up in order to get something else.

Some of you may now be inclined to believe that somehow the cost is incurred because there is always someone else involved. Therefore by becoming completely self-sufficient in producing things you need, you may succeed in making things costless.

Let us suppose that you have had enough of polluted civilization, and bid a farewell to arms and the abyss of the discontented world. After 90 days aboard a makeshift raft you reach an uninhabited island somewhere in the South Seas. There is a tropical jungle filled with edible fruits. Fish are abundant along the shores. Overwhelmed by the beauty of this paradise, you climb up the hill and release a sigh of happiness and excitement. One thing is certain, though, if you sit on top of the hill and keep watching the sunset and seagulls, there will be no meals prepared for you. Without minimal intake of meals you will soon die, and you didn't come to the island to become a fossil to be dug up by future archaeologists.

Soon you are compelled to begin building a foundation for subsistence living. You have given up all the gadgets and appliances which you used to buy from other people. Therefore, there are now no costs payable to other people. But there are still things you need. You decide to make a shelter in a cave. Unfortunately, there are no open caves around. You spend the next two days digging. You have acquired a shelter at a *cost*; namely, you have bought the shelter with two days' toil and sweat or in exchange for two days of leisure. It did not come as a free good.

Fruits are abundant in the jungle. There are neither poisonous snakes nor dangerous insects hiding behind the trees. Fish are so plentiful that you can catch them easily with your hands. Assuming that you can remain perfectly happy with a diet of only fruits and fish, the cost of meals approaches zero. It is not quite zero because you still have to pay the cost of labor in getting up and making trips to and from the jungle and the seashore. Despite the superabundance of nature-made foods all around, the real cost in the sense of pain, disutility or hardship will significantly increase if you catch yellow fever but still have to force yourself to get up and find a meal for the day.

What about the air you breathe on the island? This is indeed a free good because the supply of fresh, clean air—relative to your demand for it—is infinitely large. The air is always there to breathe, and it comes to your mouth effortlessly. A thing becomes a free good if and only if its supply is so large relative to one's demand for it that it can be made available to a person consuming it without any effort or work. Air on a tropical island is a free good, and a free good does not motivate a question of *economizing*. Therefore, air on a tropical island does not interest economists. On the other hand, clean air in cities is a scarce (economic or nonfree) good, and hence becomes an object of economics.

Our proposition that "there are no free goods" seems to work well with the familiar cases of tangible goods (dried mushrooms, water-beds) and services (haircuts, housecleaning). But you may wonder if the proposition applies to those things which we normally do not associate with economics and yet for which we have a desire— such as *understanding* and *love*. The answer is yes.

The thought process called *understanding* is an economic good because the degree of understanding we can have is conditioned by the available supply of knowledge and information, things which do not exist in a vacuum. Knowledge and information are produced, cumulated, stored and transmitted through books, newspapers, libraries, schools, speeches, symposia, and memory tapes of computers, all of which are economic goods. Knowledge and information are useless unless they can be communicated, and this requires literacy or some knowledge of a language. But learning a language is a cost-bearing process.

Love is another scarce commodity. The existence of demand for commercially sold love stories is a moving testimony to the poignant truth that true love in life is rare. That which is common and abundantly available fails to arouse our attention. If love saturated your life, you wouldn't be reading love stories.

For one reason or another, many of us have a need for loving and being loved. Either way, we are bound to face economic problems. A man wants to love a woman. His first task is to find a lovable woman, and the search alone can be a costly process. After the constraints of culture, education, religion, language and nationality are determined, he realizes that the supply of potential candidates is severely limited. He finally finds the right one but, alas, she has other boy-friends. To woo her away from his rivals with dinners and gifts, the man's cost of loving will go up significantly.

A girl wants to be loved. Perhaps, thus far she hasn't had much luck. So, instead of more daydreaming, she proceeds to buy the commodity called "being loved" by spending more on clothes and cosmetics. Some girls even try plastic surgery. The first man is out —he has chronic pyorrhea. The second man madly falls in love with

her, but his love is not requited. The girl then has to pay the phone
company to switch to an unlisted number. She learns that "being
loved" is not a free good.

> From Nikita's lunch to love,
> Things you want
> Don't come cheaply,
> If you ain't no thief
> You've gotta pay the price,
> High and low.

2.

A PARROT CAN LEARN ECONOMICS

We have established that the world offers no free lunches.
Every good and service we desire and consume is obtainable at a price.
We have not yet established, however, why some goods are more
expensive than others. Why is it that a fresh, tasty donut costs only
10 cents while a diamond (nothing but compressed carbon) carries a
price tag of 10,000 dollars? To answer this question, we must
examine the concepts of supply and demand.

Suppose you are a complete misanthrope living alone on a remote mountain. Everything you consume is produced by yourself. Primitive as it is, your life constitutes an autonomous, self-sufficient economic universe. In this one man society the price of a thing you want is your effort required to make that thing available. If you have to spend two hours to capture a rabbit, the two hours of chasing is the price of a rabbit. If you are terribly hungry and love rabbit meat but the rabbits have somehow disappeared from the area, you don't mind paying a much higher price of, say, ten hours of hunting instead of two.

Your desire for rabbits refers to *demand*; the number of rabbits in the area represents *supply*. The price of a rabbit depends upon both demand and supply. If the supply of rabbits is fixed but your demand remains strong (that is, you keep eating more and more rabbits, but the remaining few have all run away to distant spots), the price of a rabbit will rise because you must spend longer and longer hours to catch the next rabbit. If your demand is rather weak (you don't particularly care for rabbit meat) but the supply of rabbits is abundant, thousands of them around you, the price will go down for you can get one easily in fifteen minutes. So, even in this one-man economic universe, the forces of supply and demand are operating.

Most of us, of course, do not live like hermits. Instead, we prefer to live in a community in which each member specializes in producing a certain line of output because long ago our ancestors discovered that specialization (or the division of labor) raises one's productivity. A community can have more foods as well as more tools if farmers concentrate on farming and blacksmiths on making tools. They would, thus, be taking better advantage of their accumulated knowledge, know-how, experiences, and various production skills, than if each person tries to make everything he uses.

This was a clever idea. However, since the farmers needed tools and the blacksmiths foods, the fruits of the community's greater output could be enjoyed only through exchange of each group's products. This was the birth of a *market*.

When there is a buyer facing a seller, you have a market. A market is a place where buyers and sellers converge and try to exchange things in such a way that after the exchange everyone is better off. If everyone is not better off, it is hard to imagine what motivated them to come to the marketplace. A farmer comes with a bushel of wheat he doesn't need and tries to exchange it for a certain tool he wants. If he finds a blacksmith offering the right kind of tool for a bushel of wheat, the exchange takes place and both of them return home more satisfied than before.

In the beginning, *barter* (the direct exchange of commodities) was used. This method was soon found to be too cumbersome and inconvenient—especially when there were numerous commodities brought to the market. You find a fellow who wants to sell what you want but what you want to sell him is not what he wants; fish begin spoil; you want to sell a horse, but he wants only half a horse, and so on.

So, our clever ancestors soon learned the virtue of using a medium of exchange called money to facilitate exchange transactions. With money, you need not waste your time desperately trying to locate the right fellow who wants to buy from you just what you have to sell and who, at the same time, wants to sell just what you want to buy. In buying you simply pay a certain money price for the thing you want. Similarly, you sell a commodity at a money price rather than in exchange with another commodity. To serve as a medium of exchange, however, money must be made of something that is easy to carry, storable, and not too abundant. Different physical objects from stones, shells, and metals to paper have been used as money. Later we shall see that in modern society money is often not even paper but rather an idea, an illusion, a metaphysical entity.

Modern economic society is a complex of markets of all sorts, large and small, visible and invisible, highly developed and relatively simple. Millions of items are produced and traded daily. Exchange transactions are, almost universally, carried out through the use of money. Some markets have clear, physical locations (supermarkets, the New York Stock Exchange), some others exist in telephone lines and teletype machines.

A high degree of specialization is practiced by the overwhelming majority of the members of society. Typically you sell your labor, knowledge and skills for wages and salaries, then spend your money income to buy goods and services in order to satiate your demand. Specialization is so complete that in an average household practically all the things you consume—from hairpins to a refrigerator—were made by those whom you don't know and will never meet for the rest of your life.

What are the sources of demand? Some demand is to fulfill our biological needs (water, foods, clothes to feel warm, and so forth). But in modern society most of our demand is sociologically derived in that it is conditioned by the culture, tradition and mores of the community in which we live. Americans like cool beer while the British like it warm. Japanese like hot sake, while Kentuckians prefer bourbon on the rocks. Farmers demand bluejeans more than do senior executives, but the order is reversed if the commodity is a Cadillac.

Our demands are diverse reflecting our tastes, preferences and values. We demand goods and services because they contain *utilities* (seeds of satisfaction) we desire. By consuming or possessing them we become satisfied. The amount of satisfaction you get from one unit of the good you buy, however, does not stay constant. If you keep buying more and more of the same thing, the utility contained in the last unit you buy tends to diminish. The second apple after lunch does not taste as good as the first. The fourth car you purchase does not excite you as much as the third, if not the first, one. For the snobs the economists call this phenomenon the *law of diminishing marginal utility*.

Note that the *marginal* (that is, pertaining to the last unit) utility of a good can be zero or even negative. Imagine what happens if you keep eating bananas without interruption from noon until the next morning. If the 68th banana makes you throw up, that means that the 68th one has a *negative utility* (or *disutility*). You become less happy by consuming more, or you become more satisfied (less dissatisfied) by eating less bananas.

Practically all goods and services are subject to this law. Even money is no exception. A ten-dollar bill means a lot more to a high school student than to a millionaire. Exceptions usually refer to abnormal cases such as the utility of heroin to an addict, and a masochist who keeps on eating beyond the 68th banana. "Power" is the outstanding exception. As we observe politicians and dictators, it is clear that the marginal utility of power never diminishes. On the contrary, it seems to increase endlessly; the more power you have, the more power-hungry you become.

Your buying is constrained by the size of your income and prices of things you buy. The dollar you spend on good A is a dollar not available to be spent on good B. So, before you spend a dollar to buy another unit of A, you had better make sure that you are getting your money's worth. If you have had lots of A already, hence the marginal utility of A is low, you hesitate to spend more money on A; you would rather spend money on B whose marginal utility for you is still relatively high. You will buy more A provided its unit price decreases, that is, you need to spend less money than before for one unit of A. In the short run people buy more of the same thing if the price gets lower, reflecting the law of diminishing marginal utility. In other words, the seller can sell more of the same good in the short run by charging lower prices. This is known as the *law of demand*. In formal language it states that the unit price of a good and the quantity demanded of the same good at that price are inversely related.

There are some situations where this law may not apply. If you are extremely wealthy, have a taste for luxury goods and associate price with quality, then you will likely buy more luxury goods at higher prices because you think—rightly or wrongly—that the rising price reflects higher quality.

Exchange requires both a buyer and a seller, and the seller represents the supply side of the market. Goods are produced and sold because there is demand for them. However, production requires the use of many resources (factors of production or *inputs*) that are not free goods. Labor, management, capital, land, technology are scarce, and the users of these resources must pay for their services in wages, salaries, dividends, interest and rent. The sum of all the expenditures on factors of production is the total cost of production. The unit price the seller charges times the number of units of output he sells at that price is total revenue. The difference between total revenue and total cost is the seller's total profit which may be positive, zero or negative. Other things being equal, the higher the price the more the seller is willing to offer. Aside from his selfish motive to make more profits through higher prices, the price of a good tends to go up as its supply increases because the cost of production rises. To supply more goods, you need more labor; to get more labor you must offer higher wages as a way of bidding labor away from other sectors of the economy. If you try to produce more corn, you soon run out of the best available lands. You begin to cultivate less fertile lands, and the cost of corn production goes up since you have to use more fertilizers to produce the same output per acre on the marginal land. The seller then is compelled to charge higher prices in supplying greater quantities of a good so as to cover the rising cost of production. "The higher the market price, the larger the quantity of a good supplied"—this is the *law of supply*.

The laws of demand and supply can explain why some things are more expensive than others. Just as it takes two to tango, it takes both demand and supply to determine the price of a good. There is a group of buyers who buy more (less) if the price gets low (high). This group is interacting with another group of sellers who supply more (less) if the price becomes high (low). If the price of apples is too high, the quantity supplied exceeds the quantity demanded, and there will be a surplus of apples. Instead of watching their apples rot, apple growers will lower the price in order to induce people to eat more apples, and in addition reduce production of apples. If the apple price is too low, there will be a shortage of apples as the demand exceeds supply. Shortage means people are getting desperate about apples, and they express their feeling by offering to pay higher prices. So, a shortage leads to an increase in price.

What the market does is to establish the equilibrium price of a good—that right price which clears the market or equalizes demand and supply so that there will be neither a surplus nor a shortage. It takes both demand and supply to determine the price of a commodity.

If demand is strong and increasing but the supply cannot increase, the price will skyrocket. If you have a craving for an apple, you are willing to pay a higher and higher price to get the last remaining apple in the store before someone else grabs it. If you are unwilling to pay a higher price, that's another way of saying that your demand is not strong enough. If people try to eat more apples than before, the apple price will go up because more apples can be supplied only at a higher cost and the sellers of apples will try to take advantage of the situation by charging a higher price.

However, the strong and increasing demand *per se* does not necessarily imply a rising price if the supply can increase quickly and sufficiently. Despite our strong need (demand) for water, water is almost a free good because of its abundant supply. In fact you are not even conscious of the strength of your demand for it. But if all the water pipes are destroyed in a major disaster, the same water can command a high price. If you happen to own the only well in town, you can make a quick fortune by selling drinking water at a high price.

When all is said and done, the whole thing looks pure and simple. The truth is it took economists a long time to figure out this simple problem. In the Middle Ages economics was mixed with ethics and religion. People would ask not why the price was high or low, but whether the price was just or unjust on some ethical grounds. Adam Smith (1723–1790) had difficulty in explaining why such a *useless* thing like a diamond could bear a high price while such a *useful* thing like water could be so cheap. The classical economists emphasized the supply side in explaining relative prices. For example, a perfect pearl costs 25 dollars, they argued, because of the costs of labor and other inputs that went into producing it. Toward the end of the nineteenth century a group of economists in Austria began to shift focus to the demand side. They counter-argued that a pearl diver dives into freezing water to harvest a pearl because she knows that it is worth 25 dollars.

It took Alfred Marshall (1842–1924) to synthesize the two schools of thought through his scissors analogy: to ask which determines the price, supply or demand, is like asking which does the cutting, the upper blade or the lower blade of the scissors. It takes, of course, both demand and supply.

Water in a city may be cheap, but if you get lost in the burning desert of Sahara, you become perfectly willing to pay a high price for a cup of cool water. A diamond is *useless* in terms of our biological needs but it has a tremendous utility, for many people, in terms of its symbolic or psychic value. This, combined with its limited supply on earth, inflates its price. If we were living on a planet made of diamond, it will be a free good. Even on this earth diamond will become a worthless mineral if there is no industrial demand for it and people become more *rational* and lose interest in its symbolism.

A diamond is expensive,
Ding-Dong cheap,
Why the prices are high and low,
If you wanna know the answer
But your bird-brain has no answer,
Just ask a moronic bird,
The parrot will tell you,
"Supply and Demand."

3.

THE QUESTION OF CHOICE

Unlike the world of magic, in our economic universe it is impossible for us to have everything we want. At best we may hope that we select those things which we *can* have in such a way that our satisfaction will be maximized. This is the question of *optimal choice* that underlies all economic problems.

We cannot answer whether the choice we make is optimal unless we introduce and specify criteria for judgment. But judgment of any sort implies a value system, and in this sense every economic decision is a value judgment.

Economics does not attempt to determine what is (morally) good or bad for individuals, business firms, and the nation. This question belongs to ethics. Economics treats the existing value system as given (or, as a datum) and on that basis tries to work out optimal solutions. To be honest, it must be admitted that this is what economics is supposed to do rather than what it does. Only the naïve would believe that pure objectivity is possible in social sciences. The nature of economic inquiry and hence the results of the inquiry are likely to be conditioned by the personal values of the economists themselves.

The consumer's choice is limited by the size of his spendable money income, and the purchasing power of his money income depends upon prices of goods and services. If your money income increases while prices remain the same, the horizon of feasible alternatives widens. But if your money income stays the same while prices go up, the purchasing power of your income diminishes and you are forced to deal with a narrower range of choices on how much of what you can buy.

The optimal combination of goods and services the consumer can choose is that combination which will maximize his total satisfaction, given his present income, the existing prices, and his tastes and preferences. Suppose you love sour bread. Naturally you proceed to buy a lot of sour bread. But certainly you wouldn't spend all your money on bread because, if you did, you could not buy anything else and you cannot live by (sour) bread alone. You must also buy gas, socks, pencils, erasers, soft drinks and so on. Depending upon your tastes, these goods have different utilities and are subject to the aforesaid law of diminishing marginal utility. Since you have a limited amount of money, you ought to pay due attention to how much utility each good has relative to its price. The thing you like most may be so expensive that buying it wouldn't leave much money for anything else.

Thanks to the law of diminishing marginal utility, if you buy more and more of the same good, its marginal utility will be decreasing. What matters is how much marginal utility you are getting out of a given good per dollar spent on the last unit of the good. The optimal (best or rational) choice is made if you pick a combination of goods such that the marginal utilities of goods per dollar spent on their last units are all the same. If they are not the same, there is still room left for getting more satisfaction by simply shifting the combination of things until they all become equal.

For simplicity, suppose you are buying only two kinds of goods A and B. The last unit of A you buy gives you twice as much satisfaction as the last unit of B. But A is three times as expensive as B. Then, per dollar spent on the last units of these goods you are getting less marginal utility from A than from B. Remembering that a dollar spent on A is a dollar that cannot be spent on B, this means that you are overspending on A and underspending on B. You should buy more B and less A. Each dollar you transfer from A to B brings you more marginal utility from B than marginal utility lost on A. The net result is that your total satisfaction increases.

As you buy more B, the marginal utility of B diminishes while that of A increases as you buy less of A. There comes a point where the marginal utility of B per dollar spent on the last unit of B becomes equal to that of A per dollar spent on the last unit of A. That's where you stop because you have exhausted all the possibilities of raising the level of total satisfaction through changing the combination of goods you buy. The combination thus arrived at represents the optimal consumer choice. If you find this too abstract and rigorous, just remember the following proposition: "You are buying the right things if you are happy with them and believe that you are getting your money's worth from each of the things you chose to buy."

If your money income goes up and the prices remain the same, this will necessitate a change in your optimum choice of goods and services. If savings have a high marginal utility, you may decide not to spend any part of your additional income. But people typically spend more as they earn more. A 10 per cent increase in income, however, will not usually be evenly allocated on all the things you have been buying. You now buy more of something and less of something else. You begin to buy some new items, and stop purchasing some others. Those goods which people tend to buy more relative to other goods when their income goes up are called *superior goods* (for example, pink champagne, caviar, a trip to the Bahamas). Those goods which people are inclined to buy less relative to other goods as their income goes up are known as *inferior goods* (potatoes, used cars, vending machine sandwiches). Changes in consumer choice brought about by a change in income are called *income effects*.

The consumer's choice is affected also by changes in prices of goods and services. If the price of coffee rises sharply, the marginal utility of coffee per dollar spent on its last unit decreases. You no longer get your "money's worth." So, unless you are unalterably addicted to coffee, you begin to drink more tea and less coffee. This is called the *substitution effect* or more simply the *price effect*. Two goods are substitutes if they provide more or less the same sort of satisfaction to the consumer. When apples get expensive, you substitute pears for apples. The inflation of beef prices induces people to buy more chicken. Note the word "substitute" does not necessarily imply an inferior quality.

Not all goods are substitutes to each other. When an increase in the quantity demanded of one good leads to an increase in the quantity demanded of another good, the two are called *complements* or *complementary goods*. A left shoe and a right shoe, gas and tires, bread and butter are examples of complements.

Price changes require substitutions of one kind or another so that the consumer can find a new optimal combination of goods and services that gives him maximum satisfaction. At the same time price changes generate a more subtle sort of effect on your real income. When the price of just about every item goes up faster than your money income, your *real income* (or the purchasing power of your money income) decreases so that you are forced not only to substitute one good for another but also to reduce your standard of living. You may still be making the same amount of money each month, but the level of your total satisfaction becomes lower than before. If the inflation is mild and restricted to only a limited number of goods you may not even become conscious of the loss of your real income. This is because most of us are conditioned to think in terms of money income, rather than real income. Consequently, when the price of toothpaste goes up, we often fail to realize that our real income has automatically shrunk slightly.

The question of choice faces a nation as well. In the short run the nation's resources are limited. The numbers of farmers, workers, technicians, engineers are fixed at a given point in time. Lands, factories, oil refineries, office buidings are also fixed.

The nation has a choice as to the contents of its short-run maximum output. If the output consists of guns and butter, the nation can choose to have more guns and less butter, or more butter and less guns. Assuming that all the resources are now fully and efficiently utilized, however, to have more guns as well as more butter is an impossible alternative in the short run. In order to produce more guns, we must transfer farmers from farms to factories and train them to become workers capable of manufacturing guns. But now there are fewer farmers available, so the production of butter will decline. Similarly, we can produce more butter by converting workers into farmers and we achieve this goal only by producing less guns.

If the nation chooses to produce more and more of one thing relative to another, there will be a price which the nation must pay. While attempting to maximize the output of guns, we will soon be forced to employ more and more resources that are ill-suited for gun production. Those who are not mechanically inclined, Quaker farmers, militant pacifists, and others who are "marginal workers" from the standpoint of manufacturing guns will be employed. Productivity will suffer and the relative cost of making guns will go up. The same thing will happen if we try to maximize the output of butter. This is known as *the law of increasing relative cost of production.*

As time passes the size of the labor force expands, more factories can be built, and technological progress will bring about better tools and equipment. In the long run, therefore, it is possible for the nation to have more guns as well as more butter. This should not convey the impression that if we just sit and wait long enough, we will be able to produce more of everything. For the nation to raise the level of maximum output, the nation's economy must keep growing, and economic growth results from capital accumulation. This means the building of a larger and larger stock of the means of production, from research labs and dockyards to trucks and highways. But capital accumulation does not occur out of thin air. Total output consists of consumption goods and investment goods. *Consumption goods* are those goods which we use up quickly for our immediate pleasure and satisfaction (soft drinks, foods, clothes). *Investment goods* are goods used to produce consumption goods or other investment goods (trucks, tractors, turbine engines). Machines and tools depreciate; so, if the investment goods we produce this year are merely to offset the depreciation of the previously produced investment goods, then there will be no net increase in the stock of capital, and the nation's economy can produce no more output than last year. The economy is at a standstill.

There is a question of choice as to the pleasure of consumption now versus later. If the nation consumes most of its output and leaves little resources to produce investment goods, its citizens may maximize their joy of consumption in the short run, but such a hedonistic way of life will cause a grave problem over the long run. Since few resources are allocated for capital accumulation, the nation's economic growth will be slow, or there may be no growth at all, or the rate of growth may even become negative. If population keeps increasing fast, the per capita output may soon begin to decrease. Your earthly pleasure *now* will force your children and grandchildren to have the lower standards of living. This is analogous to the case of an individual who decides that doomsday is around the corner and spends all his money on liquor, skiing, women, expensive clothes, and gambling instead of saving to build his assets, investing wisely, and acquiring education and skills. He may have a great time *now*, but in the event that doomsday fails to come, he will later be suffering from a much smaller income-earning capacity than he would had he been more frugal and disciplined.

A nation strives to achieve a set of economic goals such as full employment, economic growth without inflation, equity in income distribution, economic stability and security. One difficulty in formulating the nation's economic policy is that often these objectives conflict with one another. When you try to achieve one goal, you may succeed in doing so only at the expense of other goals. In fact, it is extremely difficult—if not absolutely impossible—to fulfill all the objectives simultaneously. We are once again left with the question of choice—what combination of goals should be aimed at in the best interest of the nation.

If full employment is all that matters, the job can easily be done by letting the government build 500 pyramids in the Nevada desert each year using all the unemployed workers in the country. If inflation is our sole concern, the government can prohibit any form of price increase, including wage increases, and set a stiff penalty for violations. Economic stability can be achieved by putting everyone in jail. Output may sizeably expand by forcing every worker to work 12 hours a day, 7 days a week—at gunpoint.

The task will not be quite as easy, however, if our goal is to achieve full employment without inflation, economic stability without stagnation, accelerated economic growth without the loss of freedom.

Beauty *and* obedience. Non!
A good cook *and* a good lover. Non!
Beans *or* peas. Oui!
Butter *or* guns. Oui!
"We must restrain"
Says the Economist.

4.

CAPITALISM DIDN'T DROP FROM HEAVEN

Each economic society has to devise a scheme to solve three basic, common problems—what to produce, how to produce, and how to distribute the output among its citizens. In modern history the Western countries have been developing under an economic system described by different titles: capitalism, private enterprise system, free enterprise system, laissez-faire. These names mean more or less the same thing.

Allowing for shades of differences in particular places and times, capitalism is an economic system that assumes that the best of all possible solutions of economic problems can be sought if we leave, to the fullest extent, economic decisions to private firms and private individuals, and make sure that a high degree of competition prevails everywhere. A market for each good should consist of large numbers of producers and buyers. All barriers against free entry or exit of the firms are to be removed. Since there are numerous firms competing against one another, each firm can have only a small share of the total market—so small that there is no way for a single firm to practice any form of monopolistic control.

Each good is produced in response to consumer demand. The vigorous competition among the numerous sellers tends to push its price down to the point where it is only slightly above the *average cost* which is the cost of production per unit of output. The firm's profit margin will be razor-thin and never excessive. If it becomes excessive, new firms will be attracted to enter the market and a larger supply of output will lower the price and wipe out the excess profit. If your firm alone raises the price, people stop buying from you. They switch to other suppliers who are selling the same product but have not raised their prices.

The price-lowering effect is not the only virtue of competition. If you cannot compete with price, which is already as low as it could be, you can win the game by improving the quality of the product and by increasing the efficiency of production. Greater efficiency results in a lower cost of production which in turn enables you to cut the price without suffering a loss. The other firms that are so complacent as not to follow suit in improving their product's quality and efficiency in production will be driven out of the market.

When consumer demand for a certain product increases, the initial shortage of the product raises its price. A higher price and a higher profit margin on the part of the existing firms induce new firms to come in, and the entry of the additional firms expands the total output being supplied. The forces of competition will drive the price downwards.

If people's tastes change and consumer demand shifts away from a product, the emerging surplus reduces the price and the profits of the existing firms. There will be an exodus of the firms away from the market as those firms seek new profit opportunities elsewhere.

The presumed results of the private enterprise system are almost too good to believe. The system produces more of a good if people's demand for it increases. The supply of a good will be reduced if consumer demand for it falls. The free, competitive market wipes out excess profits and forces the price to fall as low as it can in light of the existing cost of production. The free enterprise system encourages greater efficiency and production of a better quality product. This then is the best of all possible worlds where people's economic welfare will be maximized.

What is remarkable is that all these wonders result, not from the acts of a central planning agency of the government managed by omnipotent, omniscient officials, but rather from leaving everything to the private market mechanism. Consumer sovereignty is enhanced not because every producer became altruistic and selflessly concerned with economic wellbeing of the buyers. On the contrary, each seller is merely pursuing his self-interest. There is something almost magical about the private market that converts selfish motives into everyone's gain. Adam Smith called it the "invisible hand" (of God?) that guides the economy and lets the impersonal market produce the fruits of personal happiness.

That free competition performs many wonders cannot be denied. We prefer the lowest possible price of a good we want. We are pleased if the quality of the product improves. We applaud if the competitive market drives out the inefficient firms. That beautiful smile a lady-owner gives you as you enter her store may merely be a selfish means of enticing you to buy her products, but a smile is a smile, and your shopping will be less pleasant without it. However, to think that what the model of pure capitalism suggests is what has actually been happening in the West will be a gross misreading of modern Western economic history.

There is one peculiar aspect to the rule of the game under capitalism. Suppose that your firm is extremely efficient, there is no fat in the management, and morale among workers is high. You constantly strive to reduce the cost of production and the price of your product as a way of winning the competition. The other firms that are not as motivated and hard-driving as your firm lose the race and begin to drop out one by one. The number of the firms in the market used to be 50, now the number is down to 30. Soon only 10 will be left, then only 4 . . . and so on. The logical consequence of winning the competition is that your firm will become a monopolist, and the monopoly profit should be interpreted as a reward for your hard work. But this is a violation of the market rule. You are not allowed to put up barriers against the entry of new firms that will threaten your hard-won monopoly position. You are not supposed to influence the government against invoking an anti-monopoly sanction against you. The system expects you to work hard for self-interest, and yet the full fruits of your efforts are not to be enjoyed. Human nature being what it is, it is hard to believe that business firms in reality would always behave in accordance with the rules stipulated by the theoretical model of pure capitalism.

The history of Western capitalism is filled with cases of rising "monopolies" which shouldn't really surprise us. Self-interest means that, whenever possible, you are more interested in maximizing your own profits than serving the welfare of the consumers. It is simply naïve to think that the government of a capitalist country represents all people and will not be influenced by particular interest groups. It is difficult enough just to define what a monopolist is, let alone formulate a foolproof antitrust measure. Bigness of the firm *per se* does not constitute a monopolist. What looks to be a monopolist in the coal industry is actually subject to competition from the producers of natural gas. A quasi-monopoly position in the railroad industry can be broken by the rise of the automobile industry. If pure monopoly (the whole industry consisting of just one company) is rare, the question remains—when should a big firm be declared *too* big. Is it when its market share reaches 30 per cent, 50 per cent or 80 per cent?

The model of pure competition seems to fit well some sectors of the economy such as wheat production or a cluster of downtown restaurants serving short-order lunches for office workers. However, the properties of modern technology and industrial production are often incompatible with the assumptions of the model. Modern industrial production requires enormous amounts of capital expenditures and to operate at a low cost relies heavily upon mass production techniques. But these properties are all against the assumptions of pure capitalism. Entry to and exit from the heavy equipment industry are not as easy and inexpensive as opening or closing a little cornerstore. It is impossible to introduce the mass production method as long as there are numerous firms in the industry. It is not impossible to let one hundred independent companies produce cars in America today, but under such an arrangement the cost of making a car would be much higher. The competition among many firms is presumed to encourage efficiency, but in this case the very opposite would happen. A great number of automakers would cause the American economy to utilize its resources in a more wasteful (less efficient) way in producing automobiles. Technological progress in modern society demands large research and development expenditures. If each industry is split into numerous, atomistic firms, each firm is so small that it may fail to have sufficient funds to finance and promote technological research.

Capitalism as a way of life and a mode of production began first on the British Isles, with the Industrial Revolution in the latter part of the eighteenth century. It soon spread through continental Europe, the United States, and other parts of the New World. The output of manufactures rose rapidly, but in the course of industrialization capitalism was generating certain effects that were not anticipated by the initial model of the system developed by Adam Smith and other earlier writers. In coal-mining towns and around textile mills there arose a new class of people—the proletariat—

consisting of industrial workers and their families, many of whom did not quite appear to be residents in the best of all possible worlds. They were the stepchildren of the Industrial Revolution, absorbing all the toil and pain of work for economic development with low wages and long hours, before the days of the child labor laws and unions.

Capitalism as an economic system also showed a great propensity to generate waves of business fluctuations. Economic growth of the capitalist nations did not follow a smooth, linear path, instead, it moved through a sequence of cyclical variations in business activity. Booms and depressions came and went. When a depression came, it was the industrial workers and their families who were quietly forced to bear the economic and social costs of the slow-down. Unemployment was painful, and yet the laid-off workers were told that this is the way the system operates. It was believed that the course of economic development would unavoidably have ups and downs, and a recessionary period was one of adjustment before the system returned to the norm of full employment.

The history of business cycles in capitalist countries reached its climax in 1929, when the Great Depression hit the United States and quickly spread to the rest of the world. The rate of unemployment in America soon reached an incredible 25 per cent of the labor force, and the stagnation continued through the end of the 1930s. The "invisible hand" of help was not only invisible but also unavailable. The auto-corrective mechanism of capitalism had somehow vanished from the scene. If you were an adult in the 30s with six kids and you had been jobless for five years already, it would have been difficult for anyone to convince you that full employment is the norm under capitalism or that the best of all possible worlds will come by leaving everything to the private market.

People thought
Capitalism dropped from Heaven,
The faithful but jobless
Knelt in the darkness of night
To pray for a job,
Like the tribesmen suffering from drought
Who prayed for new rains
And offered to sacrifice their maidens
To calm the wrath of God.

5.

SOCIALISM AS AN ALTERNATIVE

Each of us has a different vision of the world. Facts are seldom perceived as they are. Instead, we wear different color glasses through which things are observed, rearranged and interpreted. Empirical data is filtered through preconceptions, and not infrequently our minds see only that which they want to see. Listening to William Buckley and Paul Jacobs discuss American society, you are not sure if they are speaking of the same society.

In the mid-nineteenth century Karl Marx, who spent most of his days in the British Museum in London, wrote the monumental *Das Kapital* in which he expounded a theory of capitalism radically different from those of earlier writers, and which became a Bible for those who advocate socialism as an alternative form of economic society. Today, more than a century later, the ghost of Marx still haunts us.

Capitalism, according to Marx, is doomed and is destined to be destroyed not by the invading barbarians from without but rather by the seeds of self-destruction and inner contradictions embodied within itself. How did he arrive at this conclusion? The following is his vision of capitalism.

Human history has been the history of the class struggle. In each society there were always two opposing classes of people—the oppressors and the oppressed, the exploiters and the exploited. The masters pitted against the slaves in the ancient world, the feudal lords against serfs in the Middle Ages are cases in point. In the age of capitalism the class struggle becomes one between the capitalists and the proletariat. Each economic system rests upon a certain mode of production which in turn determines the predominant pattern of economic, social and even political life. According to Marx it is the economic system that, to a large extent, molds human consciousness— not the other way around. Under capitalism the capitalists and the proletariat are the protagonists, and all other groups of people in society play only peripheral roles.

Capitalism is an economic system that allows for the private ownership of properties. Property rights entitle the owner to a legitimate claim over all the output produced through the use of his properties. The man who owns a highly productive machine may be an all-time playboy or an imbecile; still he, the owner, is allowed to take all the return on the machine. Capitalism is a system under which goods are produced for profits. Whether goods produced for private gain also fulfill people's needs is incidental.

Capitalists are those who own the means of production but, as a rule, do not themselves engage in productive activity. The actual work is done by the proletariat who, nonetheless, have no claim to the very output they produce since they do not own the means of production.

No market value is created without application of human labor. If a good commands a price in the market, that price reflects the labor that went into producing it. Coal buried deep in the ground has no market value; it acquires value only after a coal miner digs it and ships it to a factory. Labor is the only ultimate source of generating the worth of anything that has been produced. In this sense everything produced belongs to the workers who performed the actual job of producing it.

Suppose there is a factory that employs 10 workers and produces each day an output worth 100 dollars. All the output belongs to the workers, but they get back as wages only a fraction of 100 dollars. The factory owner pays each worker, say, only 1 dollar a day. There is a surplus of labor; a number of the proletariat are begging for jobs outside the gate. If one of the workers asks for higher pay, the capitalist-owner fires him and replaces him with another worker willing to do the job at 1 dollar a day. Total daily wage cost is 10 dollars. The difference between the worth of output produced and the wage cost (which in our example is 90 dollars) is called the *surplus value*. The capitalist is naturally interested in maximizing the surplus value which represents his private gain at the expense of the proletariat.

There are two ways to increase surplus value. One way is to lower wages as much as possible. Other things being equal, the lower the wages the higher the surplus value. The capitalist gains by exploiting the workers, but this is a perfectly legitimate rule of the game. You can, however, go only so far under this approach. If the wage keeps declining and falls below the subsistence level, the workers will soon die, and you cannot exploit the dead. They must at least be kept alive to serve your interest.

Another way to increase the surplus value is through productivity gains. More machines and equipment per worker as well as the introduction of new technology will raise the labor productivity and hence the total output per day. At a given level of total wage cost, more output means more surplus value—provided that the price of the product does not fall. However, there is no automatic assurance that this second and more positive-sounding approach will result in the capitalist's greater private gain. A larger output may be cleared only at a lower price. Now, besides the wage cost, the high costs of machines, equipment and technological research must be deducted from total revenue. Since other capitalists are also striving to achieve greater productivity gains, the competition may become more and more cut-throat. Your firm cuts the price to sell more output, the rival firms follow suit which in turn forces your firm to cut the price again, and so on. The rising cost of new machines and technology and the falling revenue more than offset the fruits of productivity gains.

As long as competition remains keen, this second approach will likely lead to a falling rate of profit. The only sure way to transform productivity gains into the capitalist's private gains is through developing a monopolistic control over the market. Each capitalist now faces a strong temptation to employ whatever means available (dumping, fraud, conspiracy) to increase his market share. Some succeed in becoming monopolists; those capitalists who fail and go bankrupt join the industrial reserve army of the unemployed.

Capitalism accelerates capital accumulation and economic growth as the capitalists try to expand their means of production for their own gains. But, the internal contradictions of the system become increasingly visible as the country moves onto a higher stage of industrialization. Economic development proceeds along with the never-ending impoverishment of the working class. Real wages continue to fall. The falling profit rates will make the capitalists' behavior more frantic and irrational. Big firms grow bigger by swallowing smaller ones, and all the industries follow the inevitable path toward monopolization. Society then becomes polarized between the rich few and the proletarian masses. With social and political tension mounting, there finally comes a point when the whole system will explode in an uprising of the oppressed. The old system will be dissolved, and instead a new era of socialism arises under which there will be no more class struggles, all the means of production will be collectively owned, and goods will be produced for needs rather than for private profits.

We must bear in mind that Karl Marx was writing more than a century ago. In his days, even in England, labor was abundant and cheap. What would today be shocking working conditions were then ubiquitous in industrial towns and coal mines. Marx's vision of capitalism and predictions today seem detached from reality and almost absurd. Your reaction would perhaps have been far less critical had you looked back into history from 1935.

In the Western world, the rate of profit has not shown any clear, downward trend. Real wages have definitely been rising. Many industries have shown a tendency toward fewer firms but not quite toward complete monopolization. A political revolution that gave the *coup de grace* to capitalism took place in Russia, an underdeveloped economy relative to other Western countries, whereas the logical place for that upheaval would have been England, the oldest and most mature capitalist society. In the Marxian model the proletariat, who make up a majority in society, become poorer and poorer; but one is puzzled because they somehow continue to retain sufficient purchasing power to buy the ever-increasing output the capitalists try to sell for profit.

To say from these observations that "Marx was all wrong" is not to do him justice. A fairer question will be: "What would have happened to Western capitalism in the total absence of counter-measures and new institutions such as the system of counter-cyclical monetary-fiscal policies, social security, labor standards laws, anti-trust laws, the unemployment compensation system, the rise of the public sector and the like that have been built into Western countries since the 1930s?" In the absence of these, many of Marx's predictions as to capitalism's tendencies would have been more accurate. To put it differently, the structural changes in the Western economies over recent decades testify to our tacit acceptance of some, if not all, of Marx's prognoses of capitalism.

Socialism is an alternative form of economic organization that men have devised. Like capitalism, it did not drop from heaven. Many countries have already been practicing it for varying lengths of time. Socialism may become a reality through a variety of ways. Violent revolution is one way. Choosing it through a democratic process is another, as happened in Chile in late-1970. The Eastern European countries went socialist after World War II not because their peoples chose the new system. Russian tanks rolled in and imposed it unilaterally at gunpoint.

In its pure form socialism is an economic system that promises to cure all the evils of capitalism and provides a design from which to build a rational, humane society. In a pure socialist state private ownership of the means of production is banned. Instead, the means of production are collectively owned by everyone through the State. The private market—the heart of capitalism—is no longer relied upon in solving economic problems. Since there are no private firms, there will be no profit motive. Production will be guided in accordance with people's needs.

In capitalism the greed, selfishness, and short-sightedness of the capitalists who control the firms cause excess profits, business fluctuations, and exploitation of the working class. In socialism the government's economic planning replaces the private market and competition among private firms. The Central Planning Board of the State designs a blueprint for all aspects of the nation's economic activity—what to produce, how to produce, for whom to produce—and determines wages, salaries and prices of all goods. The experts who run the Board are the men who know what people (should?) want, and plan production accordingly.

In socialism there are no class differences, no exploitation of one group by another, and everyone works for the collective good of society. Therefore (by definition?) there will be no struggle between management and workers. Workers' complaints will be settled under internal grievance procedures within each firm. Labor unions, consequently, lose their *raison d'etre*.

It is conceivable that socialism may well function in a small, simple society where a few goods and services need be produced, and people are communally minded as well as homogeneous in terms of their culture and tastes. However, if a nation has a large population with diverse tastes and preferences, and its complex and advanced economy has to produce millions of different goods and services, it would indeed be a herculian task for the Central Economic Planning Board, with or without computers, to direct production of the right outputs at the right prices, and the allocation of the nation's resources in the most efficient manner.

Allowing for variations among the socialist states from Red China's militancy and fanaticism to Yugoslavia's more relaxed approach, being a socialist country in practice typically means that the communist party takes over the political and economic control of the nation, and economic activity is guided by a series of (long-range) economic plans. Socialism has demonstrated its capacity to promote industrialization, and many (less developed) socialist economies have been growing faster than the underdeveloped countries outside the communist bloc.

There seems to be a common tendency among the socialist nations to put relatively more emphasis than in the West on education, medicine, public health, social security and investment goods. On the other hand, people are required to swallow the leftist ideology as the only acceptable dogma, and their freedom of thought and expression is suppressed, if not completely obliterated. Consumer goods generally lack variety and are of lower quality relative to the Western products. Planning errors and wrong pricing that result in misallocation of resources are not infrequent. Lack of incentives among workers appears to be a common problem facing the socialist planners. The theory of socialism notwithstanding, the Berlin Wall and the steady exodus of refugees from mainland China to Hong Kong also provide striking evidence that socialism is not the best of all possible worlds.

There are some leftist ideologists who hold that the secret police, government censorship, concentration camps for political

prisoners and other shadowy aspects of the socialist states have
nothing to do with true socialism. This argument, however, borders
on sophism and is no less absurd than saying that depressions,
unemployment, economic insecurity, inequity in the income
distribution have little to do with true capitalism because those
things would not happen if capitalism is functioning as it is
supposed to function.

> There are two ways to freedom,
> One is to go to Amerika
> An' get fired by a capitalist
> To enjoy freedom of being jobless,
> Another is to go to Russia
> An' buy a copy of *Pravda*
> (Which means Truth!)
> To enjoy freedom
> Of reading the censored news,
> To think that
> A systems change
> (If not systems analysis)
> Will bring bliss to the world
> Is as naïve as to hope
> That a switch to a second woman
> Will let you live happily
> Ever after.

6.

THE MIXED BLESSING OF THE MIXED SYSTEM

Prior to 1929 it was widely held in the West that in the long-run full employment is the norm under capitalism. This striking optimism was based upon the then popular belief in the Say's Law (after a French economist, Jean Baptiste Say, 1767–1832) which says "supply creates its own demand." The central idea of this law is that as goods go through different stages of production from the purchase of raw materials to the shipment of finished goods to the final market, enough payments are made for all factors of production involved (wages, salaries, rent, and so forth) so that the total purchasing power thus generated constitutes sufficient demand to absorb all the goods produced. Workers, craftsmen, landlords, delivery men and all others who contribute to production and were compensated for their contributions will spend their incomes; and their total spending is presumed to be sufficiently large so that all the goods the economy has produced will be sold out. Due to market imperfections of one kind or another surpluses or shortages with respect to some particular goods might arise, but for every partial surplus there will necessarily be an offsetting, partial shortage. According to the law, it is therefore impossible for the system as a whole to suffer from a general glut or overproduction.

The market disruptions reflect the undergoing adjustments of those partial surpluses and shortages, and the associated unemployment is transitional and temporary. Competition prevails both in the products market and the resources market. Labor is mobile and there is no organized attempt at intervention (say, by labor unions) to make adjustments in wages. If the supply of labor exceeds demand for it, wages will fall sufficiently so that the firms will begin to hire more workers and full employment of the existing labor force will be restored. If the prevailing wage rate is 35 cents an hour, it means that the worth of your labor is only that much. You may not like it and decide not to work, but that is *voluntary* unemployment. You have only yourself to blame for being jobless.

If we assume full employment and a boom as the existing condition of the economy, Say's law becomes a tautology. The level of demand for output is so high that all the goods produced are cleared off the market, and this is another way of saying that "supply creates its own demand in such a way that total demand equals total supply." However, to hold that demand created by supply is *always* high enough to avert recessions and unemployment requires a religious faith in the divine tenacity of the private enterprise system.

The laissez-faire doctrine received a devastating blow when the Great Depression began in late-1929 and lasted through the decade of the 1930s. The Depression was brought to an apparent halt with the outbreak of World War II, but it is interesting to ask how many more years it would have taken the U.S. economy to make a complete recovery, had there been no war.

The Depression gave birth to the so-called "Keynesian Revolution" in economics with the publication in 1936 of the *General Theory of Employment, Interest and Money* by English economist John Maynard Keynes (1883–1946). Throughout the postwar period we have been living under the influence of Keynesian economics in one way or another.

Keynes demonstrated that it is a myth to think that a capitalist economy, when left alone, will always operate at full employment. He showed that it is perfectly possible for the economy to be trapped in a less than full employment equilibrium over a long period of time. The Keynesian system may be outlined in the following manner.

The level of employment is positively correlated with total output produced by the economy. In order to produce more goods and services the firms must employ more labor. The firms will hire less labor if the output to be produced is smaller. Output is produced in response to demand. Therefore, the level of total demand determines total output produced as well as total employment. If we are interested in raising the level of employment, the key to the solution is to increase the level of total demand (total spending on current output).

Assuming a *closed economy* (no trade relations with the outside world), demand consists of three categories: (1) consumption expenditures (on foods, clothes, appliances); (2) private investment expenditures (on new plants, machines, equipment); (3) and government expenditures (on tanks, highways, parks).

People spend on consumption out of their income. The relation between levels of consumption and income is called the *consumption function*. Suppose people spend ¾ of each incremental increase in income on consumption. (In Keynesian jargon you say the *marginal propensity to consume* is ¾.) Then, each increase in any form of spending will generate demand that is larger than the amount of the initial increase in spending. For example, you sold a piece of equipment priced at 100 dollars to a company. The company's spending of 100 dollars becomes your additional income of the same amount. (Note that spending and income are the same thing, depending upon which side you are on.) You spend 75 dollars out of 100 dollars on a new suit. The tailor spends 56 dollars and 25 cents (¾ of 75 dollars) on a new chair for his living room. The furniture dealer spends 42 dollars and 19 cents (¾ of 56 dollars and 25 cents) to have his car fixed, and so on.

The mathematically-inclined reader can easily figure out that if this process continues, there will eventually be a total demand (spending) of 400 dollars, generated out of the initial 100-dollar increase in the business firm's spending. By the same token, if the level of investment expenditures falls by 100 dollars, that will lead to a decrease in total spending by 400 dollars. These *multiplier effects* are applicable to any kind of additional increase (or decrease) in expenditures. The multiplier analysis helps to explain why we have business fluctuations and why things in the economy tend to develop in a cumulative fashion.

The sum of all expenditures by the consumers, businesses and governments—subject to the multiplier effects— is the *aggregate demand* which determines the level of output and hence the level of total employment. The presence of unemployment implies that the aggregate demand is deficient relative to the supply of labor. So, if full employment is desired, we must raise the level of demand. If the demand from the private sectors (consumers and businesses) is insufficient, the level of government spending ought to be raised to fill the gap between the present aggregate demand and that aggregate demand which is required to achieve full employment. It might be said that the impact of the Great Depression was so severe that the pump-priming under the Roosevelt Administration was too modest to initiate a major recovery and it took the enormous, military expenditures during World War II to pull the economy out of the depth of the Depression.

The type of economic system prevalent in the Western world during the postwar period has been described as a mixed economy. It refers to the death of the laissez-faire philosophy, the co-existence of the private and public sectors, a much greater role and responsibility expected of the government in the nation's economy affairs, and a serious concern with full employment and economic growth as the nation's objectives.

In the case of the United States the private sector accounts for about 73 per cent of the economy and the public sector (federal, state local) 27 per cent. Private enterprise is upheld as a matter of principle. Free competition in the market is encouraged as the best approach to enhance consumer sovereignty and the efficient allocation of resources. However, few people today seriously believe that all the nation's economic objectives can be fulfilled by leaving everything to the private market. The government readily and deliberately invokes monetary as well as fiscal policy measures to correct the (wrong) direction in which the private sector might be moving. We have today such built-in stabilizers as the progressive income tax system, social security, the unemployment compensation system, and the welfare program. We have far more knowledge and information about the economy, far more effective policy tools to cope with the problems now than before World War II. Thanks to Keynesian economics, we now have a deeper and more sophisticated understanding of macroeconomics, that is, analysis of aggregate behavior of the economy. We know what causes a depression and how to avoid it. In fact, it is extremely difficult for economists today to imagine the United States again experiencing a major depression approximating that of the 1930s.

The overall performance of the "mixed" economy since World War II has been impressive. In the United States (as in other Western countries) the trend of economic growth has been sustained. The real income (or the standard of living) of the average household has been steadily rising. Nonetheless, the picture is not all favorable. After the age of laissez-faire, the Depression, World War II and the Keynesian

Revolution, we are still in no position to declare that we have finally discovered the road to the best of all possible worlds. The mixed economic system, operating within the framework of (broadly defined) Keynesian economics, has been unable to solve the problems of inflation and inequity in income distribution.

Inflation—or continual increase in the cost of living—creates many problems. Every inflation reduces the purchasing power of a given money income. If the prices continue to rise fast, the fixed-income groups and those whose money incomes increase slowly will be hardest hit. With their now reduced real income, they can buy less goods and services while those whose money incomes manage to grow faster than prices can consume more than before. This is a case of silent but forced income redistribution resulting from inflation.

Compare the following two scenes: (1) a young man breaks into an old lady's apartment and steals her valuable antique chair; (2) a young man who received a wage increase goes to an antique shop and buys a beautiful chair which was brought in by a retired, old lady who sold it to pay her ever-rising rent.

Note what has happened is the same in both cases, namely, the old lady's chair is now possessed and enjoyed by the young man. However, transfer of the chair was carried out by a criminal act in scene one, whereas the same act in scene two was accomplished by inflation.

Inflation also chips off the real value of your savings. A 5 per cent increase in the cost of living reduces the true worth of your 100 dollars saved to 95 dollars. This is little different from someone stealing 5 dollars from your purse. But, if inflation is the thief, it is difficult to capture and bring charges against such an invisible criminal. If the bank pays interest at 4.5 per cent, the 4 dollars and 50 cents your deposit collects is not enough to cover the loss of real value of your savings. In other words, you are subsidizing the bank!

Besides the grave question of inequity, inflation may destroy the economic health of the nation. If all of us (consumers and producers) anticipate a secular (persistent, long-lasting) inflation, our behavior would become more speculative and haphazard, less restrained and cautious. The cumulative effect of such collective behavioral change upon the nation's economy will be an adverse one.

On the other hand, there is a school of thought that favors (mild) inflation. It is held that inflation stimulates investment as the business firms anticipating higher prices at which they can sell their products in the future will be induced to spend more on new plants and equipment. More investments add to capital accumulation which in turn leads to economic growth. The standards of living can ultimately be raised only through sustained growth of the economy. In this sense, inflation may be viewed as a quasi-tax to stimulate economic growth. Like any other tax, inflation, as it takes away a part of your purchasing power, hurts a little in the short run. But this special kind of "tax" stimulates economic growth and thus will bring back to you a bonus in the form of a larger real income over the long run. According to this school of thought, then, inflation is justified as long as the "average" household's real income keeps rising.

This sort of argument may remain persuasive as long as inflation proceeds at a moderate pace (2 to 3 per cent per annum), but in recent years the U.S. economy has been experiencing the sort of inflation that runs faster (5 to 6 per cent) than the rate of increase in the "average" household's money income. In 1970–1971 the trotting inflation was combined with an alarmingly high rate of unemployment; thus, the American public was presented with the worst of all possible combinations.

The traditional theory of inflation holds that inflation is a phenomenon that occurs when aggregate demand exceeds aggregate supply. In other words, too many dollars are chasing too few goods. If the economy is operating at less than full employment, an increase in spending will lead to an expansion of output. But if all the resources are fully employed and people's money income keeps increasing, an increase in their spending cannot cause output to rise. The excess demand over supply translates itself into rising prices. According to the traditional theory, then, as long as there is unemployment (indicating that the nation's resources are not fully utilized), inflation is not supposed to occur. The truth of the matter is that inflation *and* unemployment have coexisted in recent years in the United States.

The traditional theory which puts emphasis on excess demand has been called the "demand-pulled" theory of inflation. In contrast, the more recent theory, referred to as the "cost-pushed" theory, argues that prices go up because the rising costs of production push them upward. Labor unions are the villain in this theory since they keep demanding a rate of wage increase hardly warranted by the rate of increase in labor productivity. The union spokesman would respond that their wage increase is not inflationary, on the contrary, the wage increase is to adjust for the rising cost of living. The implication is that inflation is started first by someone else, and that someone else is the companies which raise their prices and hence inflate the cost of living. The company spokesman would reply that they are forced to raise prices because of the rising wage cost. Everyone is pointing his finger at somebody else, and the usual rule of thumb in a puzzle like this is that the truth lies somewhere in-between. A situation of this sort is neither purely demand-pulled nor cost-pushed. Both elements are present. It is one thing for a company to raise its price because wages have gone up, whether the company can get away with the price increase is another matter. The fact that many companies keep raising prices indicates that demand, in general, is strong and rising.

The modern, advanced economy (such as the United States) may be characterized as inflation-prone. Billions of dollars are being spent on defense. Large-scale public expenditure need at all levels never diminishes. We have become far more welfare-oriented than in the past. The social security program, the unemployment compensation system and the like have become built-in. The recent fad of counter-culture notwithstanding, the overwhelming majority of Americans are as materialistic as ever. They love to buy goods and appliances. All these help maintain a high level of aggregate demand —a setting conducive to inflation.

On the supply side, the economy has undergone significant institutional and structural changes. Major industries are dominated by a few, large corporations that are powerful enough to manipulate their markets to varying degrees. Unlike the model of pure capitalism, prices of many goods no longer respond sensitively to the shifting conditions of supply and demand. Many strong unions manage to maximize wage incomes of their members at the expense of nonmember workers and consumers at large. Many modern products are highly sophisticated and complex, and the pace of technological innovations is rapid. To manufacture them requires a number of highly trained (and retrained) personnel whose supply does not always catch up with the fast-shifting demand. Labor is not as mobile as it should be. The Seattle-based engineers, laid off as a result of a major defense cutback, could not easily pack up and go to Alaska, even if jobs are available there. Thus, the pockets of unemployment emerge and persist while the nation continues to experience inflation.

As a country becomes more affluent, the demand for products of service industry (medicine, recreation, travel, education, arts) will increase. The trouble is, service industry tends to be labor-intensive, and its productivity cannot go up as fast as in the manufacturing industry. In fact, in service industry a "productivity gain" is often synonymous with deterioration of quality. You wouldn't particularly appreciate a barber who shows off his greater "productivity" with high-powered clippers by cutting your hair in 15 seconds. Even if a college professor now teaches 1000 students per academic year instead of 500, you hesitate to judge that he has become twice as "productive" as before. The rising demand for services, combined with their supply which fails to expand as fast, inevitably inflates their prices. This is why price of a haircut, medical fees, tuition, service charges of all sorts have been rising. One way to stop the rise, which is not in accord with the life style in an advanced country, is to have no desire for those services. Today the cost of hospitalization per day can be 100 dollars or more. Americans thus face a grand paradox: their country has become so affluent that they cannot afford a hospital bed.

Some economists hold that inflation is a global phenomenon and we might as well learn to live with it. The recent experience of the mix of conspicuous inflation and a conspicuously high rate of unemployment in the United States suggests that the problem is not quite that simple.

One thing is certain. It is not impossible for the government to invoke a drastic, deflationary policy in order to bring the inflation to a complete halt. But this can be done only at a terrible price. The rate of unemployment may reach 15 per cent or even 20 per cent. On any ground, its social and economic costs will be totally unjustifiable, like killing a patient to cure his disease.

Besides inflation, the mixed economy has been unable to solve the problem of inequity in the income distribution. The high pressure economy notwithstanding, a significantly large number of Americans continue to be left out of the main stream of economic progress. They are the unskilled, the technologically unemployable, the untrainable, the marginal workers, the minority groups, the alienated, who remain poor, add to social tension and urban crises, and fail to receive the fruits of modern technology and the fantastic productivity of the American economy.

Some people maintain that the problem of "structural unemployment," pockets of poverty, the "other America" is nothing new, it has always existed in the past, and the only difference is that we are now far more socially conscious of the problem than before. We may appreciate this remarkable complacency, but their view hardly adds to the solution of the problem.

Thirty-five years after the publication of *General Theory of Employment, Interest and Money*, it is now clear that Keynesian economics is no panacea. Keynes turned Say's law around and argued that it is demand that creates supply. By now we know that this is only a partial truth. If every demand creates its own supply, that is, every increase in spending leads to a corresponding expansion of output, then there should be no inflation. The truth of the matter is we have been witnessing a secular inflation.

Keynes showed that the invisible hand was a myth and proposed a visible hand of a more active, manipulative economic policy. However, his visible hand has failed to touch the untouchables in

American society. The inequity in income distribution continues to be an unsolved issue.

Perhaps in the near future there will be another Keynes who will revolutionalize our economic thought in such a way that Keynesian and post-Keynesian economics that have been the conceptual foundation of the postwar mixed economy will look as obsolete and absurd as Say's law does to us now.

> A superstition is a religion
> You don't believe in,
> Past beliefs turned out to be myths,
> Present beliefs may be all fallacies,
> Our mixed economy seems mixed up,
> But we can't figure out a better way,
> Help us, Oh Lord,
> Send us geniuses by the dozen.

7.

IS PUBLIC DEBT BAD?

The government purchases a portion of the nation's output of goods and services to carry out its projects, from defense and diplomacy to highway construction. As a rule the government does not generate its own income by engaging in actual production of goods and services, instead it collects taxes from people and business firms, and spends the tax revenue on what has been produced by the private sector. For example, tanks as well as the toilet-paper used in the White House were manufactured by some private companies.

When total government spending equals total tax revenue in a given fiscal year, the government is said to have a balanced budget. If tax revenue exceeds government spending, the government has a surplus budget. On the other hand, the excess of government spending over tax revenue results in a deficit budget toward which many of us show an allergic reaction. It is widely held that there is something intrinsically evil and undesirable about a government deficit. In part this is the effect of the magical word "balanced" as many people associate it with things that are good and virtuous such as "balanced" diet and "balanced" personality. The mind's reflex suggests that what is not "balanced" must be bad.

Suppose we make it absolutely mandatory for the government to balance its budget every fiscal year. Under this rule the government is compelled to increase its expenditure at the time of inflation and boom because the tax revenue will go up along with the upswing of business activity and this must be matched by an increase in government spending. Otherwise there will be a surplus in the budget, which violates the fiscal rule. In a recessionary period the government is required to reduce its spending in order to adjust for the shrinking tax revenue due to the downswing. In both cases the government's fiscal action will accentuate—rather than mitigate—business fluctuations. An increase in government spending at a time of inflation will add to the overheating of the economy, and a decrease in government spending during a recession will only contribute to a further cumulative downfall of the private sector. Given the objective of economic stability without unemployment, these are the exact opposite of what the public sector is expected to do.

A modified version of the balanced budget doctrine holds that the government budget ought to be balanced over the long run and not necessarily every year. Deficit budgets in recession years are permitted provided they are offset by government surpluses during the boom period. Unfortunately, since the 1930s we have not had a chance to conduct a historical experiment to see if this modified doctrine really works because, boom or no boom, the Federal government has been under constant pressure to run deficits, mainly on account of the astronomical expenditures to finance occasional hot wars as well as the perpetual cold war.

"Is debt bad?" If you ask a man in the street this, chances are he would say "yes." If you proceed to ask him another question, "Is credit good for the economy?" he would likely say, "Of course, it is. Credit stimulates our economy." But this is a contradiction because debt and credit are the same thing—every debt implies someone else's credit. Much of the confusion that surrounds the problem of public debt stems from a frequently used analogy between private and public debts. Many of us show a Puritan complex in saying that private debt is bad because it means that you are living beyond your means, and the same is true with public debt.

Unfortunately, this contention does not apply even to private debt. To say that private debt is bad and hence should be discouraged is tantamount to denying the entire financial apparatus of the private enterprise system. If no borrowing is allowed, the business firms must finance their capital expenditures out of their internal savings, and this imposes a severe restriction upon their capacity to grow. All the commercial banks, savings and loan associations and other financial intermediaries would lose their *raison d'etre* and have to be dismantled.

The irony is that a person who contends that private debt is bad is probably living in a heavily mortgaged house. Few of us buy houses with cash. The practice of buying durable goods on credit is widespread. It would be an awkward rule to require each individual to finance his purchase of goods and services strictly out of his current income. Under such a rule, when your child falls critically ill, you cannot call a doctor or send the child to a hospital because that will necessitate expenditures beyond your current income. Similarly, you may have to postpone buying your own house till well past your retirement age.

Whether a particular personal debt is good or bad depends upon your health, income, occupation, and what the borrowing is for. Likewise, while it would be a sign of mismanagement if the firm's routine transaction expenditures are financed through borrowings, it is perfectly rational for the firm to finance its long-term investment expenditures through credit, provided that the investment plans are sound.

An analogy between private and public debts is misleading because the two are not really comparable. It is said that excessive debts will force individuals and firms to go bankrupt; but this cannot happen to the government since it is empowered to tax citizens as much as necessary to retire the outstanding debts and, in the worst situation, even to print money as the last resort. In contrast, individuals and firms are not authorized to do the same for the purpose of paying off their private debts.

A more useful analogy would be that public debt is like a person borrowing from himself. A federal debt means that Americans are borrowing from themselves. The probability of the federal government going bankrupt is no more likely than that of a man going bankrupt as a result of borrowing too much from himself. The equivalent of a private bankruptcy can occur to the government only should it become unable to meet its debt obligations to foreign nationals or governments. For example, because the U.S. government somehow cannot pay back its debt to a foreign state, it forfeits a part of U.S. territory used as collateral for borrowing from that state. This, however, is a purely hypothetical and unrealistic situation.

It is held that public debt is bad because it means that the present generation is trying to *live off* the future generations. This view is more misleading than enlightening. Much of the outstanding federal debt today is a carry-over from World War II. The real burden of the debt incurred during the war was absorbed by those who lost their lives and became crippled in fighting for freedom; because of their sacrifices we now continue to live in a free society. We are in no position to blame *them* for leaving us with the debt burden.

By the same token it cannot really be said that we are now trying to live off the generations of our children and grandchildren. At least in theory, everything the government does is in the interest of the nation. The main reason why the total federal debt outstanding shows no sign of shrinking is the continuing defense spending of staggering proportions. To the extent that the defense spending is necessary to buy "peace" and "freedom" (though admittedly many of us are getting to feel increasingly unsure about this thesis), we cannot really say who is living off whom. If this country gets destroyed, there won't be much benefit left to "future generations" of Americans. It is not impossible for *us* to retire the now outstanding debt in a short span of time by drastically raising taxes and imposing upon ourselves the rule of severe austerity. Such an approach would most probably cause a major depression, and the burden of such a disaster will befall not only us but also future generations.

It is argued that public debt is inflationary. This argument is valid if the economy is operating at full employment and the government, without restraint, tries to finance its ever-increasing expenditure by printing money or borrowing directly from the Federal Reserve Bank (which is essentially the same thing as printing money). But this is not what the government typically does.

A deficit budget usually means that the Treasury issues and sells government bonds in the private sector to raise additional revenue to fill the gap between government spending and tax revenue. Each dollar thus collected by the government corresponds to a dollar less available in the private sector. In a recession, when there are plenty of idle investible funds in the private money market, debt financing by the government is "good" for the economy. The government is trying to stimulate a stagnant economy—a task which the private sector is failing to do—by increasing its purchase of goods and services while not raising taxes in order to avoid a further shrinkage of purchasing power in the private sector. A public debt in this case means activation, through fiscal action, of money which otherwise would remain idle. The closer the economy approaches the state of full employment the more complicated the impact of the   government's deficit financing would become. Even at full employment the deficit budget *per se* is not necessarily inflationary, provided that every deficit-financed portion of government spending is matched by a corresponding, sufficient decrease in spending in the private sector due to the money shortage following the Treasury's sale of government bonds. If such a decrease fails to occur and the level of spending in the private sector remains as high as before, then the deficit budget will add to the inflationary pressure of the entire economy.

We cannot view public debt as good or bad in the same way that a little man who owns a cornerstore worries about his personal finance. The responsibility of the government in modern society and the impact of the government's fiscal policy are totally incomparable and vastly more complicated. The public debt policy has far-reaching effects upon the condition of the entire economy. To ask if public debt is good or bad is to miss the point. It is more important to examine what is happening to the economy under a particular public debt policy and to ask what will be the consequences if an alternative policy is pursued.

Ronnie the shopkeeper
Had a fall
He refused to see a doctor
'Cause he had no money.
Leaving wife an' children in misery,
Ronnie the Happie went to Heaven
Having fulfilled his motto,
"Debt is bad."

8.

MONEY FANCY

Children think that money comes out of banks. When they grow up, many of them continue to think that the banks keep enough "cash" to match their deposits. This happens to be a useful myth. In general, enlightenment is better than ignorance, but in this case the myth is what is needed for a successful working of the monetary system.

In the early 1930s, panicked by the spread of the Depression, people rushed to the banks to cash their deposits. Since there was not enough cash kept in the banks, the whole banking system collapsed despite President Roosevelt's plea that "the only thing we have to fear is fear itself." The same thing can happen even today. The system assumes that people will not simultaneously march to the banks and convert their deposits into cash. The system works because people think it does. If people lose faith and act accordingly, the system will disintegrate in the manner of a self-fulfilling prophecy.

Anything can serve as money if it may be used as a medium of exchange, a standard of value, a way of storing value and a means of deferred payment. Money is defined technically as the currency in circulation (outside commercial banks) and demand deposits (checking accounts) kept at commercial banks. Some economists prefer to include time (savings) deposits also as money. In the technical definition time deposits are not included because they are not as liquid as demand deposits. While you may cash your demand deposit anytime, the same is not true with time deposits. A bank imposes restrictions on withdrawal from time deposits, and is not obliged to accept withdrawal on demand—though this rule in practice is often waived for small savers. The currency inside commercial banks is not counted as part of the money supply in order to avoid double counting. If you deposit a twenty-dollar bill in your checking account, you have merely converted the form of money from a currency to a demand deposit. To count the bill, now in a teller's hand, as well as a new deposit is to count the same twenty dollars twice.

The definition of money, like definitions of many other things in life, is rather arbitrary. Besides demand deposits and the currency in circulation, there are many other things that may properly be called near-moneys. For example, short-term Treasury bills, grade A commercial papers and drafts are, in many ways, not much different from demand deposits.

Many people associate the currency in circulation (paper money, coins) with "money." But the currency in circulation accounts for only about 25 per cent of total money supply in the United States. Most money consists of demand deposits which are but little books with figures written in ordinary ink. In a way the monetary system works like magic. You think money is there, but what is there is merely a bunch of tiny paper books. Somehow the system works, as long as people keep trust in it.

The amounts of particular paper moneys and coins rise and fall, depending upon people's preferences. If the Philadelphia mint is cranking out a lot of quarters, it is not because the government wants its citizens to carry more quarters, but because people are *demanding* more quarters—perhaps as a result of a greater use of vending machines and parking meters. Suppose people need more quarters. They go to cornerstores and change dollar bills into quarters. The stores soon run out of quarters and the storekeepers go to local banks. The local banks then run out of quarters. They get new supplies from the Federal Reserve Bank which in turn asks the mint to manufacture more needed coins. Notice that people merely changed the forms of money they carry. Shiny coins coming out of a mint do not represent an increase in the supply of money in the country.

Commercial banks use deposit money to issue loans. They try to make profits by charging higher interest rates than those paid on deposits. There are many other institutions such as savings and loan associations, insurance companies, and investment banks that also function as financial intermediaries. But commercial banks are unique in that they are the only ones, under the law, capable of *creating* money.

Suppose you are an American exporter and have just earned 100 dollars; the next day you deposit the entire sum at your Bank A. The bank is obliged by the law to maintain the *required reserve*, expressed as a percentage of total demand deposits kept at the bank. (The requirement also applies to time deposits, but the percentage is so small that we may ignore it in our analysis.) Assuming that the required reserve ratio is 20 per cent, Bank A can issue a new loan of 80 dollars on the basis of your new 100 dollar deposit. Let us suppose that the borrower from Bank A deposits his 80 dollars in his Bank B. The reserve at Bank A now goes down to 20 dollars (100 minus 80), 20 per cent of your initial deposit of 100 dollars. Note that your deposit of 100 dollars is still there at Bank A. Now, Bank B will issue a new loan of 64 dollars (80 per cent of 80 dollars), and the second borrower deposits his 64 dollars at his Bank C, and so on. If this process continues, a chain of new demand deposits emerging at commercial banks will add up to 500 dollars (5 times as much as the initial deposit). In other words, the *system* of commercial banks (not just an individual bank) is capable of creating new money through the fractional-reserve mechanism. Money creation is not possible under the 100 per cent reserve system which requires a bank to keep a dollar of reserve for each dollar being loaned out. The financial intermediaries other than commercial banks cannot create money since they are not allowed to open and maintain demand deposits.

The money-creating capacity of commercial banks adds to the flexibility of the nation's money supply. At the same time, because of their unique legal rights, the banks' behavior may exert adverse effects on the economy. Consequently, commercial banking is regulated by the central banking authority which in the United States consists of 12 Federal Reserve Banks scattered throughout the country. The concern of the central bank is to control and adjust the supply of money, depending upon the condition of the national economy. Federal Reserve Banks have three major tools for their monetary policy: the required reserve ratio policy, the discount rate policy, and the open-market operations. When too much inflationary pressure is building up in the economy, the required reserve ratio is raised (say, from 20 to 25 per cent) so that in the chain process of money creation each bank can issue a correspondingly smaller loan. The ratio may be raised so high as to force banks to terminate issuance of new loans or even to call back the old ones in order to meet the new, higher ratio requirements.

Practically all major commercial banks belong to the Federal Reserve Banking System, and the member banks are entitled to borrow from the Federal Reserve Bank in the same way an individual may borrow from a commercial bank. At the time of a credit squeeze demand by the commercial banks for credit from the

Federal Reserve Bank will naturally rise. The latter may raise the discount rate on its loans to commercial banks as a way of discouraging member banks from obtaining more credit than is deemed desirable.

When the economy shows a recessionary tendency, the Federal Reserve authorities lower the required reserve ratio and the discount rate in order to expand credit as a stimulant for the stagnating economy. It is generally agreed, however, that these policy tools are relatively more effective as anti-inflationary measures than as devices to combat a recession. As a common saying goes, you can pull a string but not push it, or you may lead a horse to water but cannot make him drink. The point is, the lowering of the reserve ratio and the discount rate will make the terms of borrowing easier and more attractive, but this alone will not necessarily let the business firms and individuals borrow and spend more actively.

The third tool of monetary policy is the open-market operations. The open-market operations committee of the Federal Reserve Board may sell or buy government bonds in the private sector. At the time of inflation the committee sells bonds as a way of squeezing excess credit out of the private sector. In recession the committee reverses its course and buys bonds so as to supply additional credit to the private sector. The open-market operations should not be confused with the Treasury's issuing and selling government bonds. The latter refers to financing of deficits in the federal budget. The open-market operations committee does not issue new bonds; it sells and buys *old* bonds as part of the nation's monetary policy. Thanks to the fractional reserve system under which commercial banks operate, the committee's sale of a 100 dollar bond to a commercial bank leads to a more than 100 dollar decrease in credit available in the private sector. The amount of reserve at the commercial bank which bought the bond goes down by 100 dollars, but this means (assuming that the existing required reserve ratio is 20 per cent) the basis upon which the system of commercial banks could create as much as 500 dollars of deposit money is now gone. If the open-market operations committee sells the bond to an individual or an institution outside the system of commercial banks, the same result will follow, providing that the purchaser makes payment for the bond by writing a check against his demand deposit kept at a commercial bank. After the check is cleared, the commercial banking system has 100 dollars less reserve and the system's money-creating capacity has shrunk by 500 dollars. Similarly, the open-market operations committee's purchase of a 100 dollar bond from the private sector enables the commercial banks to expand credit by an amount much larger than the price of the bond.

The basic aim of monetary policy is to keep an adequate supply of money in the nation. To combat inflation, the existing policy tools are invoked in such a way that the money supply will decrease, and the tight money will lead to higher interest. The rising interest rate has a deflationary effect in general, since people and institutions tend to borrow less at a higher interest rate, as well as a credit-rationing effect, in that only those firms which have the most productive investment projects are persuaded to borrow. To cope with recession, the monetary authorities manipulate the policy tools so that the nation's money supply will increase along with the falling interest rates.

Today's monetary system is called the *managed currency system* because the money supply is adjusted at the discretion of the monetary authorities whereas in the past (before the Great Depression) many countries were operating under the gold standard system which ties the money supply to the existing stock of monetary gold in the country. Today the U.S. dollar is not at all backed by gold. The worth of your 10 dollar bill has nothing to do with how much, or little, gold is left at Fort Knox, Kentucky or in the basement of the Federal Reserve Bank of New York.

The views of economists on the effectiveness of monetary policy have gone through considerable vacillations over the past half a century or so. Before the Depression monetary policy was believed to be very efficacious in solving the nation's economic problems. In those days economic policy meant primarily monetary policy. In the 1930s the faith in monetary policy was replaced by the cult of fiscal policy. During the postwar period the majority of economists view fiscal policy and monetary policy as complements, since both are necessary, useful and effective—depending upon the particular circumstances—in achieving the nation's economic goals.

Controversy still persists as to the relative importance of money in a modern economy. A group of economists, known as *monetarists,* insists that there is abundant historical evidence to prove that an increase (decrease) in money supply leads to an increase (decrease) in output and employment. If this is true, the task of economic policy will be reduced to one of simply adjusting the money supply in the *right* way. This is presumably all it takes to accomplish economic growth at full employment and without inflation. Much controversy centers around the interpretation of the alleged historical evidence. Some economists, for example, suggest that the apparent covariance between money supply and output-employment merely shows that an increase (decrease) in money supply is not the cause of, but rather is caused by, an increase (decrease) in output and employment. The monetarists believe that it is the other way around.

A system works
'Cause you think it does
Money, like love, is an illusion,
You think it's there
An' trust money-mongers,
As a lover trusts his lover,
An' that's what
Makes the system tick.

9.

GOODS AND BADS

The dollar value of total output of goods and services produced each year by the nation's economy is called *GNP* or *Gross National Product.* When GNP is getting bigger, we say the economy is growing. If GNP is expanding faster than the population, per capita output also increases. This is assumed to signify that the average citizen's standard of living is rising.

In by-gone centuries when poverty was a norm, production of anything would be good and contributory to the raising of people's

61

material well-being. When you are starving, you aren't too particular about the choice of foods, you appreciate any additional supply of food. When few shelters are available, you would welcome any new dwelling units. A shack is better than nothing at all. This is the origin of the word "good." The time was when any goods produced were "good."

The trouble with GNP is that it includes everything that has been produced, and says little about qualities or kinds of goods being produced. GNP does measure the nation's capacity to produce, but greater capacity does not necessarily imply a higher quality of economic life in the nation. To advocate a bigger GNP without qualification is like measuring a child's "growth" solely on the basis of his weight and height. A child who grows taller and gains weight without an end will turn out to be a monster.

In the age of affluence we are surrounded by thousands of goods from stereo sets to electric toothbrushes. The average American today is neither starving nor cold; on the contrary, he is overfed and works in an overheated office in winter. His problem is not "Where can I get another cake of soap?" but rather "What kind of soap is more area-effective for my armpits?"

The market for consumer goods assumes a form characterized as *monopolistic competition*, namely, many firms that produce the same category of goods fiercely compete against each other through vigorous advertising and other promotional measures, and each firm tries to establish a monopoly position by differentiating the external appearances of its products as a way of capturing the fancy of the consumers. More effort goes into changing shapes of bottles and boxes than in improving the true quality of the product.

Product differentiation, mixed with aggressive advertising, may succeed in monopolizing a large segment of the consumer population. Some people buy only Bayer aspirin, as though that were the only kind available, despite the fact that the chemical contents of all aspirin tablets are federally regulated. You may always buy Dial soap as if the soap industry were monopolized and Dial the only kind manufactured. The firm's quasi-monopoly position is a precarious one. Consumers are fickle, and the other competing firms may come up with *better* products any day. A sense of insecurity drives management to pour more millions of dollars into television commercials.

A spokesman for Madison Avenue would say: "We live in the age of opulence. We must distinguish between our *needs* and our *wants*. Most of our basic needs are already fulfilled. The question is what people want, depending upon their tastes and preferences. The advertisers are not trying to force people to buy anything. People choose what they want. As a matter of fact, many of the products we promote fail. Who is to say what's good for consumers?"

Persuasive as it is, the trouble with this argument is that it ignores the impact of a particular social and economic system upon the wellbeing of individuals and assumes that the consumers have the true autonomy of choice and decision making.

In promoting its products the firm will unavoidably aim at the masses. The truly educated and the culturally sophisticated constitute only a small fraction of society. To play safe, each firm will market what it thinks will appeal to the largest number of consumers. The advertisers will do almost anything to sell. If sex is found to be an effective sales-producer, it is readily mixed with any product you can name from a fat Buick to a Virginia Slim. Mass culture will flourish, and this is what people presumably want. The cult of deodorants and the vulgarization of sex are what people supposedly believe in. Anyone who faintly suggests the importance of a cultural elevation of society will be criticized as manifesting an elitist mentality. Rich Americans must travel abroad to realize that French peasants eat much tastier bread than the mostly air-filled supermarket bread of America and that there are better alternatives of dining pleasure than Howard Johnsons and Doggie Diners. We are all creatures of circumstance. American consumers may have abundant freedom to be a part of plastic culture but have far less freedom to get out of it.

The curse of opulence is that one more appliance in the household wouldn't make a housewife much happier. But we continue to think in terms of the nineteenth-century mentality and listen to the message of a by-gone era—"Produce, produce and thou shalt be saved."

The increasing number of goods being produced are of the kind that leaves us wondering whether producing more of them really adds to our well-being. In fact, the present-day GNP includes many goods which should more aptly be called "bads." Spending on tranquilizers, psychiatrists, divorce lawyers, riot squads, junk mails, unsolicited phone calls, drug clinics, napalm, H-bombs and the like all goes into GNP statistics. Yet greater production of these indicates the rising misery and frustration of people. If GNP is meant to be an index of economic welfare, these items ought to be deducted from—rather than added to—the statistics.

Some of you may object by saying that tranquilizers and psychiatrists, in and of themselves, are not "bads" because they are there to eliminate or alleviate pain and frustration. This interpretation, however, misses the point. Anything you name is produced in response to someone's demand. Heroin may be classified as "good" because without it an addict will be in greater misery. Napalm is "good" because some think that, without it, Americans will more likely be enslaved by the dark forces of communism. In other words, all goods are (intrinsically) "good" since they were produced to satiate someone's need or desire. But this is to confuse the issue. "Bads" should be defined as goods of such nature that an increase in their production indicates rising discontent and economic ill-health of the nation. If GNP measures the "positive" economic health of the country, then spendings on tranquilizers and psychiatry ought to be deducted. With sleeping pills many Americans remain less unhappy, but being happy is not quite the same thing as not being unhappy. A sound, happy individual with no need for pills should not be equated with a man whose staying not unhappy requires a lot of pills.

Both production and consumption involve external economies (benefits) as well as external diseconomies (costs). If introduction of mass production techniques sizeably reduces the cost of steel, the steel users outside the steel industry will benefit from it even though they did not pay for the development of the technique. This is an example of external economy of production. If a factory pollutes a nearby lake and the rest of society has to absorb the cost of losing a clear lake, that is an instance of external diseconomy of production.

Similarly, the consequences of private consumption are not necessarily confined to the domain of life of the consuming individuals. Sensible parents who spend a good deal on education and love in the family are likely to produce children who will later be spreading happiness to other people in society, and this is a case of external economy of consumption. On the other hand, if you are an alcoholic and often disturb the peace of your neighborhood, you are exemplifying an external diseconomy of consuming alcohol. Chances are, your neglected children will grow up to become law-breakers, and the rest of society will have to pay the cost of maintaining the police and jails.

In past centuries the population was small and production on a modest scale so that the external economies of production and consumption as a rule far exceeded their diseconomies. People looked at the stream of goods coming out of the front end of a factory with excitement, and ignored the ugly debris being dumped into a lake behind the building. No matter, there were still many other clear lakes untouched by the industrial civilization! The mode of consumption was modest enough so that any diseconomies of private consumption were not yet excessive enough to be felt by everyone. Garbage left by a horseriding cowboy wouldn't be too conspicuous in the middle of the Nevada desert.

Joseph Schumpeter (1883–1950) used the concept of "creative destruction" in explaining economic development and business cycles in a capitalist society. To him, capitalism is an economic system whose dynamic movement is promoted by the entrepreneurs, that group of restless individuals who are never satisfied with the status quo and who design and innovate new products, new machines, new ways of doing things. Innovation destroys the old market equilibrium as machines and tools become obsolete. But this is creative destruction. This is how a capitalist society moves onto a higher stage of development.

As we come to the age of mass consumption, it is not "creative destruction" but rather "destructive creation" that characterizes the mode of production. In the name of creating goods and services to serve the needs of people, so much of our environment is being destroyed, often in an irreversible way. Trees are cut to provide room for new highways, bulldozers tear up the natural landscape to build more houses, many species of whales have already become extinct, mercury and DDT are poisoning our seafoods, and so on.

If the environmental destruction continues at the present rate, the coming of doomsday for *homo sapiens* is only a matter of time. In fact, it has already arrived at some spots on earth. Groups of school children in Tokyo have fallen on the playgrounds, overcome by the poisonous smog. In the same metropolis traffic cops at busy intersections have to return to their police boxes every half-hour or so to breathe pure oxygen from a tank.

Should we then give a *coup de grace* to the cult of GNP and terminate the game of growthmanship? That, unfortunately, will not solve our problem. Nothing is wrong with GNP or modern technology *per se*. Most of us prefer material comfort and wellbeing to poverty, and it takes production of goods and services to get out of the trap of scarcity. The curse of mass consumption has little to do with the question of comparative economic systems. The Russians have reportedly been suffering from their own environmental crises. Too many cars with combustion engines per square mile cause smog in any city, Russian or American.

The ecological crises are, to a large extent, the result of our misuse of technology and resources and a reflection of our slowness in cultivating a new ethos applicable to the post-industrial society. What is needed is a fundamental reorientation of our minds so that we can make a clear distinction between "goods" and "bads" and regulate production as well as consumption (if necessary, with militancy) to make sure that their diseconomies be held at the absolute minimum. The cost of environmental protection will be high, and the prices of consumer goods will rise accordingly. But that is the unavoidable, high cost of living in a post-industrial society.

To say
A poor saint can be happy
Is a lot of nonsense.
He is happy
Not because of
But in spite of poverty.
Goods are good,
Bads are bad,
The road to happiness is simple
Produce good goods only.
Pack in Saturn-rockets
Polluters and beer-can droppers,
An' send 'em away
Into outer space.

10.

IS COMPETITION GOOD?

Production of goods and services generates incomes that must be distributed as profits, wages, salaries, interest, and rent to compensate for the services rendered by the various factors of production. In coping with the question of income distribution (namely, who gets which slice of a pie), it is generally believed that the system of free competition among those who own the factors of production is the most rational and effective way to get the best results.

If the demand for chemical products exceeds their supply, the free market signals the emerging shortage by raising their prices. The higher prices induce the producers to increase the supply of chemical products, and this necessitates, among other things, hiring of more chemical engineers. In the context of free competition the laws of supply and demand operate in the market for factors of production just as well as in the products markets. Given the shortage of chemical engineers, the price of the knowledge and know-how of chemical engineering will rise as the market's way of increasing the supply of chemical engineers. Their rising salary will make the field relatively more attractive to science students in colleges and universities. Dynamic and efficient firms can afford to offer yet higher salaries to snatch the best engineers from other, less productive firms. According to the market principles this is *good* because the best engineers receive the highest compensation and end up being employed in those firms where their talents can best be utilized. What is true for chemical engineering is true for all other factors of production. In other words, the free competitive market will achieve the optimal distribution of incomes and the efficient allocation of resources.

Suppose there are two individuals, Brown and Jones. Brown is a top executive at a large corporation, drawing an annual salary of 60,000 dollars. Jones is a clerk in a small firm, and earns 6000 dollars a year. In a general way, we know why the difference between the two men's incomes exists. Brown has managerial talent of the sort which is an extremely scarce commodity, whereas Jones is an average individual with an average mentality. The difference occurs because there are too few Browns and too many Jones relative to the demand for the kinds of services they can offer. However, to answer a more particular question—"Why does one get 60,000 dollars and the other only 6000 dollars?"—we must go beyond the usual laws of supply and demand, and the economists' answer is often based upon the marginal productivity theory of wages.

If a firm hires more and more workers while all other factors of production than labor remain fixed, total output of the firm will increase; but the amount of increase in output resulting from employing the last workers (called *marginal output*) will eventually begin to fall. The marginal output of the 500th worker in a factory with 100 machines, each designed to be operated by one worker as a norm, will be much smaller than that of the 50th worker. This reflects the *law of diminishing marginal returns* which says that if you increase one input while all other inputs are fixed, total output will increase, but at a decreasing rate (the marginal output attributable to the variable input will be diminishing). This law is believed to apply to all factors of production. For example, if we fix the land and the amount of fertilizers used but increase the number of farmers, the additional output of foods due to the last farmer we hire will become smaller and smaller. Soon there will be so many farmers standing around that no open space will be left for plants to grow. If the law did not exist, it would be possible for us to produce all the foods required to feed the world's population out of a small pot by using enormous amounts of fertilizer.

If the worth of marginal output per day of the 50th worker is 25 dollars, it pays the firm to hire him provided that his daily wage is anywhere below 25 dollars. The firm will hire more and more workers as long as the marginal productivity of labor is larger than the wage and will stop hiring when the two become equal. What is the same thing, according to the *marginal productivity theory of wage*, the productivity of the last worker hired tends to equal the wage rate for him as well as for all other workers doing the same job. If your daily wage is 30 dollars, that means your marginal productivity is worth 30 dollars. If you demand more than 30 dollars, you won't be hired, and without employment you earn no wage. Where labor is abundant relative to capital, the marginal productivity of labor becomes low, and hence the wage too will be low. The converse situation occurs when labor is scarce relative to capital.

General Motors may pay an executive 60,000 dollars a year because his activity is worth that much to the company, or to put it differently, it is believed that in his absence the company's revenue will go down by 60,000 dollars or more. Aside from whether what the company believes is true, the company will not pay him such a salary unless it thinks that the executive is worth at least that much. Some executives do get fired when the company finds out that their worths were grossly overestimated.

The marginal productivity of a man in a competitive, economic society refers to his productivity in producing anything for which there happens to be demand. A popular singer or a movie star can earn a fabulously large income because there are millions of fans willing to pay for the tickets to consume the particular kind of entertainment produced by the particular individual. An increase in demand for popcorn will induce an increase in the supply of corn. But in the case of a popular entertainer, the supply is absolutely fixed. There is one and only one Frank Sinatra. So, the price of the commodity can go up without a limit, depending upon the intensity of demand.

If you say that something is "wrong" with a society which allows a silly singer to earn an income much larger than that of the head of State or a college professor, the orthodox economists would reply that you are trying to impose your values on the rest of society—you are telling other people what they should or should not want. However, it must be remembered that the system of free competition itself represents a value according to which whatever happens through the free market mechanism is believed to be necessarily "good" for society.

The marginal productivity theory takes as given the existing pattern of income distribution, and then explains why some people are rich and the others poor. But, the theory does not quite explain why the present pattern of income distribution came into being and whether or not the present pattern is truly optimal with respect to the goals of society.

All men are equal before the law, but we are definitely not equal in terms of prenatally determined talents and mental capacities. Some are born smarter than others, and many high paying occupations in modern society require the sort of intelligence which one's postnatal "effort" and "hard work" cannot cultivate. If you were a fool, you could not understand differential calculus, and without a knowledge of differential calculus you could not become a highly paid engineer. So, there is a question of equity that ought to be answered: Is it fair to have a system which differentiates people's incomes on the bases of those factors for which they are not responsible?

If you went to Princeton and the Harvard Law School, a stream of high income is more or less assured you for the rest of your life. However, only a very few of us manage to go to Princeton and Harvard. In life nothing succeeds like success, and nothing fails like failure. Rich parents can afford to give the best education to their children who as a result will earn high income. On the other hand, those who are trapped in the pit of cultural deprivation find it enormously difficult to break out of the vicious circle between poverty and low education. The equity in the presently observed distribution of income in society is more apparent than real to the extent that the competition in the process of social and economic ladder-climbing is not fair and there are visible as well as invisible barriers against some individuals' attempts to realize their full potentials.

Historically, it has been noted that the free-market economy tends to give rise to income gaps of significant proportions. Some get much richer than others, but the marginal utility of 100 dollars to a man who makes 200,000 dollars a year may be a small fraction of that to a man whose annual income is only 3000 dollars. Given the fact that the law of diminishing marginal utility applies to one's money income, we face a problem of how to maximize total wellbeing of the entire society with regard to income distribution. The greater the inequality in income distribution, the higher the probability that society's total welfare can be increased by redistributing income through a nonmarket method, such as taxation. The utility of 100 dollars transferred to a family with six starving children would likely more than offset the disutility of a millionaire who has lost his 100 dollars.

The system of free competition as applied to the labor market dictates that the firms should fire marginal workers, and this is said to be good because competition encourages hard work and productivity, and discourages mediocrity and laziness. This system may be good from the standpoint of private firms but not necessarily good for society as a whole. What's good for General Motors may not always be good for the country. The argument runs as though the fired marginal workers will vanish from the earth. The truth of the matter is that they don't vanish from the earth but continue to be a part of society. Marginal workers may migrate to marginal firms, but the competition will force the marginal firms to go bankrupt and all the former employers and employees of those firms now jointly march to skid row. A private gain thus creates an additional problem with which society has to cope.

The system of free competition also tacitly assumes that all members of society are fond of competition. This, however, is a rather unrealistic assumption to make about human nature. Some of us work hard, independently of how much money income we make as a result. It is doubtful that a 200,000 dollar executive will work only half as hard if his salary is reduced to 100,000 dollars. At the same time, there are many others who do not like competition and prefer a quiet, simple life to a grinding work load mixed with ulcers. No matter how good-natured, honest and well-meaning these people might be, they are *persona non grata* from the standpoint of the competitive system, and are discriminated against accordingly in terms of their income shares.

Any economic system is man-made and exists presumably to serve men. However, since men's desires and aspirations are not homogeneous, each system unavoidably tends to favor some and discriminate against others. More importantly, we should remember that there is nothing sacrosanct about the competitive way of solving the problem of income distribution.

Feudal lords had their ways,
Free competition has its way.
If you ain't too smart
Then do some dirty jobs,
If you don't wanna work
Social workers'll fix you.
If you ain't fond of competition,
You better move to a cuckoo land.
The system has its logic
Society has to survive,
Without some system
All will perish.

11.

FREE TRADE AND ALL THAT

If each state of the Union since the founding of the nation, had been allowed to maintain tariff walls and other barriers against free movement of goods and resources, most of us can see intuitively that America today would have been far less affluent. The United States may be viewed as a group of some 50 "nations" that have been practicing free trade among themselves, and their regional economic integration has paid off handsomely with the highest standard of living in the world.

If the principles of free trade are good for domestic trade, they must also be good for international trade. The argument in favor of free trade is based upon the *comparative-cost doctrine* initially developed by David Ricardo in the early nineteenth century. Unlike many other doctrines of the day, it has survived the test of time up to the present.

The comparative-cost doctrine holds that trade between two countries will be mutually gainful if each country exports those goods whose comparative costs are low, and import those goods whose comparative costs are high. In England, let's say, it takes 1 man-hour to produce a unit of cloth and 2 man-hours to make a unit of wine. However, in Spain 1 man-hour is necessary to produce a unit of cloth and 1.5 man-hours to make a unit of wine. Then the comparative cost of cloth is lower in England than in Spain, while the comparative cost of wine is lower in Spain than in England. In this example, England should export cloth and import wine, and Spain should import cloth and export wine. By so doing, each country is using its resources more productively than without trade. England has a relative advantage in cloth so she concentrates on cloth, and lets Spain concentrate on wine, the product in which Spain has a relative advantage. As a result more of both goods become available in the two countries, and trade is thus mutually gainful.

What counts is the comparative cost, rather than the absolute cost expressed in some particular currency. Trade can be mutually beneficial as long as there are differences in the comparative costs, but this fact often becomes obscured when we think in terms of absolute costs, as the following analogy will illustrate.

Suppose there are a lawyer and his secretary. The lawyer can make 50 dollars an hour for his legal work. He happens to be a very fast typist, and he can earn 10 dollars an hour as a typist. His secretary knows some law and can make 5 dollars an hour by doing legal work; she is employed as a typist and can produce 7 dollars' worth of typing output per hour. If we think in *absolute* terms in this case, there should be no "trading" of works between the two because the lawyer is more productive in both legal work and typing than his secretary; he, the faster typist, should do all his typing. But this is a foolish proposition. Every hour he allocates to typing involves the loss of 50 dollars earnable through legal work. He should concentrate on legal work because that is where his comparative advantage lies. Similarly, the secretary should concentrate on typing even if her typing is slower than his.

The comparative cost is largely determined by the relative abundance of a factor of production. The greater the supply of a factor (relative to other factors), the lower the price of that factor. In a labor-abundant, capital-scarce country, labor will be cheap. The country should try to export labor-intensive products (those products whose production requires a lot of labor and little capital) and import capital-intensive goods. If a country tries to produce goods using scarce resources instead of importing them, the country is only hurting its own people. Suppose that a certain toy if made in the United States will cost 10 dollars, but the same toy if made in Hong Kong will cost only 2 dollars. Without trade you pay 8 dollars more to buy the same thing thus leaving you 8 dollars less to spend on something else. Obviously, the absence of trade lowers your standard of living. It is not difficult to imagine what would happen to the welfare of American consumers if the United States decided to stop importing coffee, cocoa, bananas, silk and other commodities in which America's relative disadvantages lie and, instead, to produce them all domestically. Americans would either be paying much higher prices, or prices would get so high that they might choose to consume less or none of those goods. Either way, they will be worse off than before.

Most of the commonly heard protectionist arguments are either total nonsense or a way of protecting some special interest groups at the expense of others, or else arguments based upon some non-economic grounds.

It is said that a high-wage country such as the United States cannot compete with countries endowed with cheap labor. Literally read, this statement implies that the lower (higher) the wages, the stronger (weaker) the nation's capacity to export. But this is contradicted by the fact that the United States, a high-wage country, managed to export some 40 billion dollars' worth of merchandise in 1970. The fallacy of this argument stems from confusion between wage rate and wage cost. In developing countries wage rates are low because of low labor productivity which in turn tends to inflate wage cost per unit of output. In the United States the hourly wage rates may be high, but high labor productivity, together with abundant capital, makes many American products highly competitive in the world market.

It is held that the flood of "cheap" foreign goods is causing unemployment in the United States. This argument ignores the fact that trade is a two-way process. The foreign countries acquire dollar exchange by exporting their goods to us. If we do not buy their goods, they do not earn dollars, and without dollars they cannot buy from us. Therefore, a reduction of our imports leads to a decline of our exports, and those Americans employed in the export industries will lose their jobs. While the problem of depressed industry, hit by foreign competition, should not be ignored, we must remember that there are thousands of Americans gainfully employed because foreigners are buying their products.

Often national security is cited as the reason for protection. It is maintained that a strategic industry must be protected because the critical dependence upon other countries for defense goods will prove fatal in a major war. This is a distinctly noneconomic argument. One cannot escape a certain air of paranoia behind an argument that assumes all our allies will suddenly betray us by going neutral or declaring belligerence against us once the war breaks out, and/or the war in question will last for years in lieu of the more likely 45 minutes under a nuclear holocaust.

Irrespective of particular arguments used, every protection implies that the protected industry is subsidized by the consumers of its products. If a tariff raises the domestic price of a protected product by 50 cents, then the consumers are subsidizing the producer by paying 50 cents extra. This is no different from the government's imposing a 50 cent specific tax and giving the tax revenue to the producer. In that event the consumers would be outraged; but the same people, when told that the tariff is protecting the American industry from foreign competition, usually remain calm, revealing the extent to which their minds have been poisoned by the disease of nationalism. Also, the rate of subsidy per unit of output is typically so small that the average consumer fails to notice it despite the fact that the total subsidy to the protected industry, collected from millions of consumers, can be enormous.

We are all for competition as long as we are not adversely affected by it. What is true for individual firms is also true for nations. It was more than a coincidence that sometime after Adam Smith (1723–1790) was advocating free trade in England, Friedrich List (1789-1846) was writing in Germany on the virtue and importance of protectionism as a way of promoting industrialization of the country.

England, though poorly endowed in raw materials, then had the most advanced economy in the world. It was most advantageous for her to export manufactures and import needed materials of all sorts from the rest of the world. From the standpoint of England it made perfect sense to argue that she should export manufactures in which her comparative advantage lay, and the other countries should export to England raw materials in which they held a relative advantage.

To Germany, then an underdeveloped country in relation to England, the free trade doctrine was a highly egotistical argument which was designed primarily to serve the national interest of England. If a country is underdeveloped and hence cannot possibly compete with more advanced countries in industrial products, free trade merely perpetuates the backward status of the country. An agricultural economy will forever remain agricultural; a country that now heavily depends upon exports of primary resources is doomed to repeat the same for good. List was the first to attack the hypocrisy of the free trade philosophy behind the mask of internationalism and to develop the strain of protectionist thought that has come to be known as the *infant-industry* or *young-economy* argument. (This is said to be just about the only justifiable reasoning for protection.)

No industry in a less developed country can grow without some protection. But industrialization is vital if the country aspires to become a socially, politically, and economically advanced state. Protection involves short-run costs in that the country has to pay higher prices for domestically produced industrial output, because of the infant stage of home industry, than if it had imported the same goods from the more advanced, foreign countries. According to the young-economy argument, however, protection is justified if there is reasonable certainty that the domestic industry will grow mature in a sufficiently short time, and the long-run (social as well as economic) gains from industrialization are believed to far exceed the short-run costs of protection.

Nonetheless, infant-industry protection is subject to abuse and failure. It may be a necessary, but hardly a sufficient, condition for successful industrialization of a country. The "infant" may refuse to grow up and keep expecting protection forever. Other industries may start demanding equal protection regardless of the prospects of their development. A protected industry may be destined to become a declining industry in the context of world trade by the time it finishes growing up. At any rate, successful industrialization requires a lot of other factors besides mere protection.

> I stand for good things
> I am for competition
> As long as I'm winning.
> I am for free trade,
> As long as I can sell my things.
> If I lose—that's bad,
> If I can't sell—that's equally bad,
> Let me make my position
> Perfectly clear,
> I stand for good things
> I stand against bad things
> At least I'm consistent.

12.

A FAVORABLE BALANCE OF TRADE

In eighteenth-century England there was a very popular politico-economic doctrine called *mercantilism*. Its main idea was that a nation's wealth and strength depend upon the stock of gold, and therefore the country should strive to export more than its imports as a means of acquiring gold from other countries paying in gold for the excess of their imports. The accumulation of gold was considered good not only for its intrinsic value but because the precious metal could be used for political bargaining purposes as well as for hiring mercenaries and purchasing strategic materials in fighting wars on foreign lands.

Some 200 years later the mercantilistic mode of thinking still lingers on in many of our minds. The average American, as he reads about an outflow of gold from the United States, feels rather uneasy, though he does not quite think that monetary gold is held by his government as a means of fighting foreign wars or that his wellbeing is determined by the volume of gold kept at Fort Knox, Kentucky.

The survival of mercantilistic thought is most evident in the popular expression "favorable balance of trade." When a country's exports exceed imports, the trade balance is said to be "favorable." The truth of the matter is that it is anything but "favorable" and should more appropriately be called an "unfavorable balance of trade."

Exports are those goods which a country produces and lets foreigners (rather than its own people) consume. Similarly, imports are those goods which foreigners produced for us to consume. A favorable balance of trade means that we are doing more work for foreigners than they for us. If the United States run an export surplus of 4 billion dollars, that implies that the United States is letting the foreigners have 4 billion dollars worth of merchandise in excess of what we are getting from them. If you know a person who always exchanges his things for other people's possessions that are worth less, you would call him a fool or a saint. Anyone who advocates a favorable balance of trade is either a fool or an anti-nationalist who thinks of the welfare of foreigners before that of his own people.

Under normal circumstances, a country cannot export more than it imports from the rest of the world. A country exports as a way of earning foreign exchange to be used to buy abroad those things which the country wants but cannot domestically produce at all or can produce only at high relative costs. If the United States maintains a "favorable" balance of trade year after year, the foreign countries soon run out of the supply of dollars they earned by exporting their goods to us. They will be compelled to pay for the excess of their imports in gold or their currencies. A chronic "favorable" balance of trade will result in an ever expanding stock of gold or holding of foreign currencies in the United States. But your economic wellbeing depends upon what you actually consume (including Danish cheese and French wines), and not upon how many tons of gold or British pounds your country has accumulated.

The United States can only continue to have a favorable balance of trade without piling up gold or domestically useless foreign currencies if foreign countries manage to acquire dollars through means other than exporting to the United States. If you examine trade statistics, you will notice that throughout the postwar period (prior to 1971) the United States has been exporting more than importing. The rest of the world has been able to buy more from us than we from them because this country has been giving away billions of dollars as economic aid and spending abroad more billions on U.S. troops and military bases on foreign soil. Since the aid money and the military offshore procurements are ultimately paid out of tax revenue, it is the American taxpayers who have been subsidizing foreigners so that they could buy more from us than we from them. And this is what a "favorable balance of trade" is all about.

Besides exports and imports, a country's international economic involvement includes other "nontrade" items such as capital inflows-outflows and unilateral receipts-payments. The total of these transactions is compiled into what is called the balance of payments. When there is a net outflow of "money," the country is said to be having a balance-of-payments disequilibrium.

Money is necessary to carry out domestic as well as international trade. For domestic trade each nation uses its own currency. Since there is as yet no single world currency for international trade, during the postwar period the international means of payments have mainly consisted of U.S. dollars, British pounds and gold. These three have been the major components of "international liquidity" or the foreign exchange reserves of trading nations.

A balance-of-payments disequilibrium leads to a depletion of the foreign exchange reserve, and this cannot go on too long because the country will eventually run out of its foreign exchange holdings and become unable to meet external payment obligations. As a short-run solution the country may borrow desired currencies from the International Monetary Fund which pools financial resources from the member countries. If the disequilibrium persists, the country, with the approval of the Fund, may depreciate its currency as a way of increasing exports and decreasing imports so that the disequilibrium will be removed. Suppose that the exchange rate between Japanese yen and U.S. dollar is 360 yen to 1 dollar. If we depreciate yen by changing the rate to 400 yen to 1 dollar, this makes Japanese goods cheaper to Americans and American goods more expensive to Japanese. Americans then can buy 40 yen's worth more in Japan for the same dollar while Japanese have to pay 40 yen more to buy the same good worth 1 dollar in America. As a result, Japanese exports to the United States will rise and her imports from the United States will fall.

The United States is in a peculiar position because the U.S. dollar is an international means of payment as well as the domestic currency. Because of this peculiar position the dollar shortage cannot be a balance-of-payments problem for the United States. It is inconceivable that the U.S. would run out of its own currency (no dollars left in America!). The often-heard U.S. balance-of-payments difficulties refer to the steady outflow of monetary gold from the country.

While American exports exceeded imports during the postwar period, the size of her export surplus has been shrinking steadily, reflecting the relative deterioration of competitive strength of American goods in the world market due to the advancement of West European and Japanese economies. In addition to the global commitments of the U.S. government causing heavy overseas expenditures, more and more American private capital has been invested abroad. As a result of all these factors, the amount of U.S. dollars held by foreign countries has been steadily increasing. Some foreign governments understandably want to convert their dollars into gold rather than building up their reserves consisting exclusively of dollars. Before August 15, 1971 the conversion could be easily carried out because the U.S. Treasury would always sell or buy gold at 35 dollars per ounce provided the seller or the buyer was a foreign central bank. The foreign countries had been buying gold from the United States and, if the trend continued, it was only a matter of time before U.S.-held gold would be completely drained off. What would it have meant? Not much. The U.S. economy would still be there just the same, producing millions of goods with its mighty technology and skills. The official belief before August 15, 1971 was that the United States would lose "face" before the world if its Treasury could not honor its pledge to sell gold to foreign countries. All this may sound silly, and the fact of the matter is it is silly. Before that date it was feared that the Treasury's inability to unconditionally sell gold will shake the world's confidence in the U.S. dollar and the resulting psychological repercussions will deal a hard blow to the international financial community. Here we see a certain split personality in action. The dollar as a domestic currency is no longer backed by gold and nobody is troubled by it, but the worth of the same dollar as an international currency was supposed to depend upon its link to gold. The worth of a dollar at home or abroad, however, has little to do with gold. The value of a dollar refers to output a dollar can buy in the United States. It is the productivity of the American economy that determines its worth.

As an alternative to the discretionary rule for the Treasury, we may raise the dollar price of gold. It was back in 1935 that the U.S. government set the price of gold at 35 dollars per ounce. In a way it is something of a cheat to continue to use the same price today because inflation since the 1930s has considerably reduced the purchasing power of the dollar. Today you have to spend more dollars to buy practically everything than in the 30s. So, the price of gold should accordingly be corrected to, say, 70 dollars per ounce. Then, from the standpoint of those countries which keep a lot of gold in their international reserves, an increase in the dollar price of gold (which is the same thing as devaluation of the dollar in terms of gold) will make American goods cheaper and hence those countries will buy more in the United States. Per ounce of gold they now can get 70 dollars worth of American merchandise instead of 35 dollars worth. The benefit of this approach goes to those nations which hold large stocks of gold, and, ironically, the list of beneficiaries includes the Soviet Union and the Union of South Africa. The foreign governments will no longer be quite as eager to buy gold from the United States as before since they now have to pay twice as high a price in dollars. On the contrary, the foreign governments will be happy to sell gold to the United States. As a result the stock of gold in America will increase, dissolving the so-called balance-of-payments difficulties.

Why isn't the dollar price of gold raised? The reason, once again, is a psychological one. Devaluation of the dollar is said to be a humiliating, embarrassing and degrading experience to the United States—the world leader, a giant in the community of nations. The explicit pronouncement of an American "failure," it is held, will touch off international disorder and cause the world economy to crumble like a house of cards. Of course, this is nonsense; but official minds do not concur.

Another alternative to solve the U.S. balance-of-payments problems is to get rid of gold completely from the international monetary system and let the freely fluctuating rates of exchange between different national currencies settle the external balance of each nation. If inflation in the United States proceeds faster than in the rest of the world, and as a result the country begins to run import surpluses, the dollar should be depreciated relative to other national currencies so that American exports will expand while her imports will fall sufficiently to correct the situation. There is nothing "shameful" about this; we are merely making an adjustment for the domestic inflation. The necessary rate changes can be implemented either by having the government follow a flexible formula or through the free foreign exchange market. In either case the changes are made without recourse to gold, a mineral with a mystical power, which has intrigued the human mind since time immemorial and with which we are, to this day, still hung up in dealing with international financial problems.

It's silly
To dig gold in South Africa
Only to bury it in Kentucky.
We should use it
To make more practical things,
Golden bridges,
Golden teeth,
Golden statues of
Nixon an' Agnew.

13.

THE SECRET OF ECONOMIC DEVELOPMENT

We tend to forget that until recently the whole world was more or less economically underdeveloped. There were always rich kings and aristocrats, but the masses everywhere—East or West—lived a life devoid of the blessings of materialism. We may call Thailand today a poor country in contrast to America's richness; before the turn of the century, however, the per capita real income of this country was not much higher than that of present-day Thailand.

In the late eighteenth century the Industrial Revolution began in the British Isles, and the waves of economic development spread to Western Europe and America. Nowadays we are so conditioned to a dichotomous view of the rich West versus the poor East that we fail to note that the spread of industrialism was uneven even within the Western world. Russia and much of Eastern Europe long remained underdeveloped relative to other Western countries.

Today two-thirds of the world population still continue to live in "underdeveloped" countries as though their economic time clock stopped moving centuries ago. The majority of these underdeveloped countries are located in the Eastern world, and despite their efforts and varying degrees of success during the postwar period we have not yet witnessed a significant closing of the income-wealth gap between the East and the West. As a matter of fact, in many areas the relative gap has been actually widening.

Per capita GNP is usually used to classify a country as rich or poor. In many ways this is unsatisfactory. Living in Vermont, you must buy a heavy overcoat and spend 50 dollars or more per month for heating in winter, and these are added to the U.S. GNP. On the other hand, neither overcoats nor heating are necessary in Samoa, and the Samoan GNP will be that much smaller. The GNP approach also tends to ignore noneconomic things of value in life. The average man in an economically poor land may still lead a culturally rich life, and he would not particularly appreciate the connotation of the word "underdeveloped." The first expression used after World War II was "economically backward." This term raised so many sensitivity issues that the United Nations adopted a new expression "less developed" which was later switched to "underdeveloped" and finally to the present terminology "developing."

Per capita GNPs among nations of the world range from somewhere above 3000 dollars down to mere 50 or 60 dollars. Those with less than 200 dollars are customarily classifed as "poor" or "developing" countries.

What are some common characteristics of the "poor" countries? A very high percentage of the total population (80 per cent or more) lives on farms. The literacy rate is critically low. There is a general paucity of skilled personnel in all fields from science to administration. The social overheads such as public schools, roads, dams, hospitals are insufficient. Capital is scarce, and labor productivity is low. Many of these countries suffer from tremendous population pressure. Total output produced may expand each year, but population keeps increasing as fast or faster, so that, on a per capita basis, the average man's lot stays the same or even worsens with time.

Thomas Malthus in the early nineteenth century expounded a theory of population according to which food production can be raised only at an arithmetic rate while population increases at a geometric rate; it is therefore a matter of time before we run out of foods to feed the world's population. He underestimated the impact of technology and scientific research that led to a continual rise in agricultural productivity in the later decades, and his gloomy prediction has not come true (thus far) in the Western countries. However, the essence of his population theory still carries much relevance to the problems of the underdeveloped countries today.

Theories of economic development abound, each emphasizing a particular factor or a set of factors, ranging from the Protestant ethic, weather, and the paucity of natural resources to the curse of colonialism, capitalist exploitation, internal decadance, and many others. Economic development is a complex process that involves political and social changes as well, and the only possible generalization seems to be that we cannot hope for a unicausal explanation of the poverty of nations. A given factor may apply to one case but not necessarily to others.

A rich internal supply of industrial raw materials appears to be a necessary (if not sufficient) condition of economic development. Yet, countries like Japan, Italy and Great Britain are heavily industrialized without being abundantly endowed with them, while many poor countries have resources in abundance within their territories. The truth seems to be that the internal availability of industrial materials is neither a necessary nor a sufficient condition.

The bigness or smallness of a country as well as the size or density of its population does not quite explain the state of economic development. The United States is a large country with a large population and is highly developed. India is also a large country with a large population, but is underdeveloped. Belgium and Holland are small and densely populated, yet theirs are advanced economies. Many small, densely populated countries in Latin America and Southeast Asia are poor. Australia and Canada are large, sparsely populated countries with high standards of living. A remarkable case is Iceland, a tiny dot in the North Sea, where the per capita real income is one of the highest in the world. One universal trait throughout the developed countries, large or small, is the high rate of literacy, and that appears to be one of the keys to economic development.

In view of the widespread underdevelopment in Latin America, one is tempted to hypothesize that the orthodoxy and conservativism of the Catholic Church, in contrast to the Protestant ethic that encourages hard work on earth as a way of fulfilling God's will, have something to do with the poverty of the region. This hypothesis, unfortunately, fails to explain the case of France, a developed and Catholic country.

Professor Alexander Gerschenkron popularized the theory of "catching up" according to which the latecomers are prone to develop fast because they have a strategic advantage in being able to borrow technology and the developmental skills quickly from the more advanced countries instead of going through a slower and more costly trial-and-error approach. The theory applies to Germany and Japan, but not to many poor countries today that are "latecomers" and yet somehow do not "catch up."

Professor W. W. Rostow wrote a stage theory of economic development which divides the process of transformation of a national economy into five stages: (1) a traditional (preindustrial) society in which economic and social organizations are conditioned by inflexible customs and traditions rather than economic rationality, the ethos of industrialism and scientific know-how; (2) a period in which such preconditions for economic growth as sufficient numbers of technicians, administrators, educators, minimum social overheads and the like are to be fulfilled; (3) a period of take-off, when the growth of the country begins to accelerate like an airplane taking-off from the airfield; (4) a period of sustained growth in which the per capita real income of the nation keeps rising steadily; and finally (5) a period of mass consumption when every household has several television sets and even imbeciles drive shiny automobiles. Useful as it is in describing the steps of transformation of a nation from a backward to an advanced status, the theory does not quite explain why some countries manage to grow rapidly and others do not.

That the Western world, by and large, has developed within the framework of capitalism does not necessarily imply that any other economic systems are not suited for the task. Today there are many socialist states that are highly industrialized. Those who are quick to point out the human costs involved, say, in Soviet development are reminded of the horrifying tales of sweat shops and child labor in the early phase of industrialization in England, and the history of slavery that casts a dark shadow over the case of capitalist development on the American soil.

A poor country is plagued by vicious circles of all sorts. The masses are uneducated and without skills, their productivity is therefore low. Low productivity leads to low income. Low income can yield little savings, the low rate of savings results in the low rate of investment and without investment the capital accumulation in the country is insufficient. An inadequate stock of capital leads to a small capacity to produce output. As a result, the nation remains poor and the poor people cannot afford to acquire education and skills.

In a poor nation too many people are tied to lands. The agricultural productivity is critically low. Foods produced by the peasants are barely enough for their own subsistence. As long as the agricultural sector is unable to produce surplus foods to feed the nonagricultural population, the country is stuck with the status of an agrarian economy. Economic development requires large numbers of factory workers, managers, accountants, scientists and others who jointly perform the task of nation-building and who do not grow their own foods.

The world has witnessed a variety of approaches to economic development. Entrepreneurship in a competitive environment has generally led the way in the Western countries. Japan's economic growth since the late nineteenth century has been blended with nationalism, militarism and strong government leadership. The Soviet Union has practiced considerable regimentation of its citizens. Most recently, Red China has been mixing frenzy with militancy in promoting her industrialization.

No matter which approach might be adopted, it seems to take several generations to transform a backward nation into a modern industrial state. The shorter the timetable, the greater the discipline and sacrifice that will be required of people. Sometimes the internal decay, corruption and disorganization after centuries of backwardness may be so thorough and profound that it will require bloody, radical measures—although there is no guarantee that such measures will bear fruit.

Unfortunate are the members of the generations before a nation reaches an advanced stage of development who must work hard, be content with a low standard of living and save what they can out of their meager incomes. Their work provides development funds so that not they but future generations will be able to enjoy the taste of affluence.

Economic development does not occur in a vacuum, nor does it blossom out of a political ideology. Rather, it is a result of people's hard work. Their spirit may be sustained by a religious faith, nationalism or the achievement orientation of their society. If the initiative is lacking, the will to develop may have to be imposed upon them by the State. It is a cruel fact of life that those who sacrifice most are to be rewarded the least. The increasing opulence of Soviet citizens today is based upon the toil of Russian peasants of past generations. Behind the affluence of present-day Japan are the haunting shadows of numerous village girls who died young of consumption after long hours of confinement in poorly ventilated textile mills.

Is economic development worth all its costs? There are moments when we wonder if there is any alternative to material civilization. The thought that perhaps there is no ultimate validity in insisting that all nations, East and West, must achieve industrialization quickly vanishes, however, once you witness with your own eyes the thousands of homeless sleeping in the streets of Calcutta or the body of an Indian girl being tossed into a stream because her father cannot afford to buy firewood to cremate her body. In the eyes of a starving child in Afganistan you do not see the glory of spiritual civilization. If the child is happy, it is not because of, but in spite of the poverty of his land. To anyone who really knows how easy it is for man's life to be reduced to one of misery, indignity and degradation in the context of economic backwardness, "poverty or wealth" is not an abstract issue of alternatives. The dilemma of affluence notwithstanding, the choice of poverty will certainly not solve human problems.

> The secret of development is
> To feel inferior
> And work like a maniac
> To catch up with the West,
> Or
> To feel superior an' build
> Tallest buildings,
> Longest bridges,
> Biggest dams,
> Heaviest tanks.
> Gunpoint is one method,
> Gradualism is another,

Calvinism may help,
Try nationalism too.
In all cases,
Forget about five-year plans,
Pick a shovel,
An' go to work.

A GUIDE TO BASIC ECONOMICS TEXTS

For more detailed studies of the topics discussed in this book, the reader must consult textbooks on introductory economics. Ten leading texts have been selected for reference purposes. This guide shows the correspondence between chapters of this book and those in the texts. Texts are referred to by authors' names and corresponding chapter numbers.

Basic Economics Texts:

Alchian, Armen A., and William R. Allen. *University Economics.* (2nd ed.). Belmont, Calif.: Wadsworth Publishing Co., 1969.

Bach, George Leland. *Economics: an Introduction to Analysis and Policy.* (7th ed.). Englewood Cliffs, N.J.: Prentice-Hall, 1971.

Guthrie, John A., and Robert F. Wallace. *Economics.* (4th ed.). Homewood, Ill.: Richard D. Irwin, 1969.

Harriss, C. Lowell. *The American Economy.* (6th ed.). Homewood, Ill.: Richard D. Irwin, 1968.

Lipsey, Richard G., and Peter O. Steiner. *Economics.* (2nd ed.). New York: Harper & Row, 1969.

McConnell, Campbell R. *Economics: Principles, Problems, and Policies.* (4th ed.). New York: McGraw-Hill, 1969.

Nichols, Donald A., and Clark W. Reynolds. *Economics.* New York:
    Holt, Rinehart, and Winston, 1971.

Reynolds, Lloyd G. *Economics.* (3rd ed.). Homewood, Ill.:
    Richard D. Irwin, 1969.

Samuelson, Paul A. *Economics.* (8th ed.). New York: McGraw-Hill,
    1970

Suits, Daniel B. *Principles of Economics.* New York: Harper & Row,
    1970.

Chapter 1   A Free Lunch for Anyone?

Alchian and Allen, 1; Bach, 1; Guthrie, 1; Harriss, 1; Lipsey and
Steiner, 1; McConnell, 1, 2; Nichols and Reynolds, 1, 2;
Reynolds, 1; Samuelson, 1; Suits, 1

Chapter 2   A Parrot Can Learn Economics

Alchian and Allen, 4, 5, 11, 12, 14; Bach, 21; Guthrie, 2;
Harriss, 14, 15; Lipsey and Steiner, 10, 11, 12, 13,14;
McConnell, 4, 26; Nichols and Reynolds, 4, 5; Reynolds, 4;
Samuelson, 4; Suits, 15

Chapter 3   The Question of Choice

Alchian and Allen, 3; Bach, 10; Guthrie, 1; Harriss, 12; Lipsey
and Steiner, 5; McConnell, 1; Nichols and Reynolds, 3, 8;
Reynolds, 1, 14; Samuelson, 2, 22; Suits, 14

Chapter 4   Capitalism Didn't Drop from Heaven

Alchian and Allen, 2, 15; Bach, 2, 25, 34; Guthrie, 17, 18, 19;
Harriss, 2; Lipsey and Steiner, 6, 7, 17, 18; McConnell, 3, 22, 35;
Nichols and Reynolds, 13, 14, 15, 16, 17; Reynolds, 3;
Samuelson, 3, 26; Suits, 6, 7, 8

Chapter 5   Socialism as an Alternative

Alchian and Allen, 25; Bach, 42; Guthrie, 35; Harriss, 37;
Lipsey and Steiner, 46; McConnell, 44; Nichols and Reynolds, 18;
Reynolds, 2; Samuelson, 42; Suits, 27

Chapter 6   The Mixed Blessings of the Mixed System

Alchian and Allen, 26, 27; Bach, 6, 7, 16, 27; Guthrie, 3, 4, 5, 28;
Harriss, 38; Lipsey and Steiner, 31, 32, 33; McConnell, 6, 12, 13;
Nichols and Reynolds, 31, 32, 37; Reynolds, 7, 8;
Samuelson, 11, 12, 13, 41; Suits, 9, 10

Chapter 7   Is Public Debt Bad?

Alchian and Allen, 24, 28; Bach, 13, 35; Guthrie, 1, 3;
Harriss, 13, 32; Lipsey and Steiner, 34; McConnell, 14, 15;
Nichols and Reynolds, 22, 23; Reynolds, 25; Samuelson, 8, 9;
Suits, 12

Chapter 8   Money Fancy

Alchian and Allen, 29, 30, 31; Bach, 11, 12; Guthrie, 6, 7, 8, 9;
Harriss, 6, 7, 8; Lipsey and Steiner, 35, 36, 37, 38; McConnell,
16, 17, 18; Nichols and Reynolds, 33, 34, 35, 36; Reynolds,
11, 12; Samuelson, 15, 16, 17; Suits, 13

Chapter 9   Goods and Bads

Alchian and Allen, 15; Bach, 26; Guthrie, 33; Harriss, 39;
Lipsey and Steiner, 19; McConnell, 7, 29; Nichols and Reynolds,
10, 11, 12, 30; Reynolds, 18, 19; Samuelson, 40; Suits, 20

Chapter 10   Is Competition Good?

Alchian and Allen, 20, 23; Bach, 29, 30, 32; Guthrie, 22, 23;
Harriss, 22, 23; Lipsey and Steiner, 23, 24; McConnell, 32, 37, 38;
Nichols and Reynolds, 7; Reynolds, 20, 21; Samuelson, 6, 27,
28, 29, 30, 31, 39; Suits, 22, 26

Chapter 11   Free Trade and All That

Alchian and Allen, 33; Bach, 37; Guthrie, 30: Harriss, 33;
Lipsey and Steiner, 40, 41; McConnell, 40; Nichols and
Reynolds, 24, 25; Reynolds, 28; Samuelson, 34, 35; Suits, 21

Chapter 12   A Favorable Balance of Trade

Alchian and Allen, 36; Bach, 38, 40; Guthrie, 32; Harriss, 34;
Lipsey and Steiner, 39; McConnell, 41, 42; Nichols and
Reynolds, 38; Reynolds, 27; Samuelson, 33, 36; Suits, 21

Chapter 13   The Secret of Economic Development

Alchian and Allen, 38; Bach, 18; Guthrie, 28; Harriss, 36;
Lipsey and Steiner, 45; McConnell, 43; Nichols and Reynolds,
39, 40; Reynolds, 32, 33; Samuelson, 38; Suits, 4

SUGGESTED READINGS

These readings were selected for those who wish to go beyond basic textbooks to explore some of the classics in the field or pursue fuller treatments of the various topics mentioned in this book.

For Chapter 1   A Free Lunch for Anyone?

Boulding, Kenneth E. *Beyond Economics.* Ann Arbor: University of Michigan Press, 1968.
Brown, Alan A., Egon Neuberger, and Malcolm Palmatier, (eds.). *Perspectives in Economics.* New York: McGraw-Hill, 1971.
Hazlitt, Henry. *Economics in One Lesson.* New York: Harper & Row, 1946.
Mundel, R. A. *Man and Economics.* New York: McGraw-Hill, 1968.
Paarlberg, Don. *Great Myths of Economics.* New York: New American Library, 1968.

For Chapter 2   A Parrot Can Learn Economics

Hutchinson, T. W. *The Significance and Basic Postulates of Economic Theory.* London: Macmillan, 1938.
Knight, Frank H. *The Economic Organization.* New York: Harper & Row, 1951.

Robbins, Lionel C. *The Nature and Significance of Economic Science*. London: Macmillan, 1932.

Robinson, Joan. *Economic Philosophy*. Garden City, N.Y.: Doubleday, 1964.

Schumpeter, Joseph A. *History of Economic Analysis*. New York: Oxford University Press, 1955.

For Chapter 3   The Question of Choice

Buchanan, James M. *Cost and Choice*. Chicago: Markham, 1969.

Gisser, Micha. *Introduction to Price Theory*. Scranton, Pa.: International Textbook Co., 1970.

Melman, Seymour (ed.). *The War Economy of the United States*. New York: St. Martin's Press, 1971.

Myrdal, Gunnar. *Objectivity in Social Research*. New York: Pantheon, 1969.

Rogers, Augustus J. *Choice: an Introduction to Economics*. Englewood Cliffs, N.J.: Prentice-Hall, 1971.

For Chapter 4   Capitalism Didn't Drop from Heaven

Chase, Harold, and Paul Dolan. *The Case for Democratic Capitalism*. New York: Crowell, 1964.

Heilbroner, Robert L. *Between Capitalism and Socialism*. New York: Vintage Books, 1970.

Ropke, Wilhelm. *Economics of the Free Society*. Chicago, Ill.: Henry Regnery Co., 1963.

Schumpeter, Joseph A. *Capitalism, Socialism and Democracy*. New York: Harper, 1950.

Wright, David McCord. *Democracy and Progress*. New York: Macmillan, 1948.

For Chapter 5   Socialism as an Alternative

Baran, Paul. *The Political Economy of Growth*. New York: Monthly Review Press, 1957.

Hayek, Friedrich. *The Road to Serfdom.* Chicago, Ill.: University of
    Chicago Press, 1950.
Lange, Oskar, and Fred M. Taylor. *On the Economic Theory of
    Socialism.* Minneapolis: University of Minnesota Press, 1952.
Mermelstein, David (ed.). *Economics: Mainstream Readings and
    Radical Critiques.* New York: Random House, 1970.
Sweezy, Paul M. *Socialism.* New York: McGraw-Hill, 1949.

For Chapter 6   The Mixed Blessings of the Mixed System

Budd, Edward C. (ed.). *Inequality and Poverty.* New York:
    Norton, 1967.
Galbraith, John Kenneth. *The New Industrial State.* Boston:
    Houghton Mifflin, 1967.
Hansen, Alvin H. *A Guide to Keynes.* New York: McGraw-Hill,
    1953.
Heller, Walter. *New Dimensions of Political Economy.* New York:
    Norton, 1967.
Keynes, John Maynard. *The General Theory of Employment,
    Interest and Money.* London: Macmillan, 1954.

For Chapter 7   Is Public Debt Bad?

Burns, Arthur F., and Paul A. Samuelson. *Full Employment,
    Guideposts and Economic Stability.* Washington, D.C.:
    American Enterprise Institute, 1967.
Economic Report of the President. Washington, D.C.: Government
    Printing Office (annual).
Heilbroner, Robert L., and Peter L. Bernstein. *A Primer on
    Government Spending.* New York: Random House, 1971.
Lecht, Leonard A. *Goals, Priorities and Dollars.* New York:
    Free Press, 1966.
Tobin, James. *National Economic Policy.* New Haven: Yale
    University Press, 1966.

For Chapter 8   Money Fancy

Federal Reserve Bank of New York, *Monthly Review.*
Friedman, Milton, and Walter W. Heller. *Monetary vs Fiscal Policy.* New York: Norton, 1969.
Hansen, Alvin H. *Monetary Theory and Fiscal Policy.* New York: McGraw-Hill, 1949.
Money and Credit; The Report of the Commission on Money and Credit. Englewood Cliffs, N.J.: Prentice-Hall, 1961.
Ritter, Lawrence S. (ed.). *Money and Economic Activity.* Boston: Houghton Mifflin, 1961.

For Chapter 9   Goods and Bads

Chamberlin, Edward H. *Theory of Monopolistic Competition.* London: Oxford University Press, 1948.
Crocker, Thomas D., and A. J. Rogers III. *Environmental Economics.* Hinsdale, Ill.: Dryden Press, 1971.
Ehrlich, Paul, and Anne Ehrlich. *Population, Resources, Environment.* New York: Freeman, 1970.
Galbraith, John Kenneth. *The Affluent Society.* Boston: Houghton Mifflin, 1958.
Mishan, E. J. *The Cost of Economic Growth.* New York: Praeger, 1967.

For Chapter 10   Is Competition Good?

Brown, Claude. *Manchild in the Promised Land.* New York: Macmillan, 1965.
Friedman, Milton. *Capitalism and Freedom.* Chicago, Ill.: University of Chicago Press, 1962.
Hailstones, Thomas J., et al. *Contemporary Economic Problems and Issues.* Cincinnati: Southern-Western Publishing Co., 1966.
Heilbroner, Robert L. (ed.). *Economic Means and Social Ends.* Englewood Cliffs, N.J.: Prentice-Hall, 1969.
Schnore, Leo F. (ed.). *Social Science and the City.* New York: Praeger, 1967.

For Chapter 11   Free Trade and All That

Haberler, Gottfried. *The Theory of International Trade.* London:
William Hodge, 1936.
Johnson, Harry G. *The World Economy at the Cross Roads.*
Oxford: Clarendon Press, 1965.
Kindleberger, Charles P. *Power and Money.* New York: Basic
Books, 1970.
Meier, Gerald M. *International Trade and Development.* New York:
Harper & Row, 1963.
Ohlin, Bertil. *Inter-regional and International Trade.* Cambridge,
Mass.: Harvard University Press, 1957.

For Chapter 12   A Favorable Balance of Trade

Balassa, Bela, (ed.). *Changing Patterns in Foreign Trade and
Payments.* New York: Norton, 1964.
Cohen, Benjamin J. (ed.). *American Foreign Economic Policy.*
New York: Harper & Row, 1968.
Friedman, Milton. *Dollars and Deficits.* Englewood Cliffs, N.J.:
Prentice-Hall, 1968.
Snider, Delbert A. *International Monetary Relations.* New York:
Random House, 1966.
Triffin, Robert. *Gold and the Dollar Crisis.* New Haven: Yale
University Press, 1961.

For Chapter 13   The Secret of Economic Development

Higgins, B. *Economic Development.* New York: Norton, 1968.
Novack, David E., and Robert Lekachman, (eds.). *Development and
Society.* New York: St. Martin's Press, 1964.
Rostow, W. W. *The Stages of Economic Growth.* London:
Cambridge University Press, 1960.
Supple, Barry E. (ed.). *The Experience of Economic Growth.*
New York: Random House, 1963.
Ward, Barbara. *The Rich Nations and the Poor Nations.* New York:
Norton, 1962.

INDEX

INDEX